Teaching En
by the Book

Teaching English by the Book is about putting great books, wonderful poems and rich texts at the heart of English teaching, transforming children's attitudes to reading and writing and having a positive impact on learning. It offers a practical approach to teaching a text-based curriculum, full of strategies and ideas that are immediately useable in the classroom.

Written by James Clements, teacher, researcher, writer, and creator of shakespeareandmore.com, *Teaching English by the Book* provides effective ideas for enthusing children about literature, poetry and picturebooks. It offers techniques and activities to teach grammar, punctuation and spelling, provides support and guidance on planning lessons and units for meaningful learning, and shows how to bring texts to life through drama and the use of multimedia and film texts.

Teaching English by the Book is for all teachers who aspire to use great books to introduce children to ideas beyond their own experience, encounter concepts that have never occurred to them before, to hear and read beautiful language, and experience what it's like to lose themselves in a story, developing a genuine love of English that will stay with them forever.

James Clements is a writer, researcher and the founder of the education website shakespeareandmore.com. Formerly a teacher and school leader in London, James works with teachers, groups of schools and education authorities in the UK and across the world to support the teaching of English.

Teaching English by the Book

Putting Literature at the Heart of the Primary Curriculum

James Clements

Routledge
Taylor & Francis Group
LONDON AND NEW YORK

First published 2018
by Routledge
2 Park Square, Milton Park, Abingdon, Oxon OX14 4RN

and by Routledge
711 Third Avenue, New York, NY 10017

Routledge is an imprint of the Taylor & Francis Group, an informa business

© 2018 James Clements

British Library Cataloguing-in-Publication Data
A catalogue record for this book is available from the British Library

Library of Congress Cataloging-in-Publication Data
A catalog record for this book has been requested

ISBN: 978-1-138-21314-2 (hbk)
ISBN: 978-1-138-21315-9 (pbk)
ISBN: 978-1-315-44896-1 (ebk)

Typeset in Galliard
by Sunrise Setting Ltd, Brixham, UK

For Mary Mann (Amberley C of E First School) and Joe Winston (The University of Warwick) – two teachers who taught me lessons that will stay with me forever.

About the author

James Clements is a writer, researcher, and the founder of the education website shakespeareandmore.com.

A respected authority on curriculum design and the teaching of English in primary schools, James has worked with groups of schools, education organisations and governments in the UK and across the world. James' key areas of interest are the development of language comprehension, building a rich reading culture in schools and innovative approaches to supporting children's written communication, and his work in these areas has received widespread attention. Prior to this, James was a teacher and school leader in central London.

Contents

Contents

Acknowledgements

It has become a bit of a cliché to appropriate Isaac Newton and say that your book was written standing on the shoulders of giants, but in this case it's true. This book exists because I've been lucky enough to read the work of giants, ponder the ideas of giants and, on occasion, swap emails or share a coffee with giants. My thanks go to:

Janet Brennan, Nikki Gamble, Deborah Myhill, Teresa Cremin, Eve Bearne, Jane Oakhill, Kate Cain, Jeremy Hodgson, Chris Winch, Sir Jim Rose, Joe Winston, David Sellens, Lindsay Johnson, and the teachers and pupils of Thomas Jones School, Margaret Meek, Mat Tobin, Ruth Leask, Gill Budgell, Ruth Miskin, Rachel Clark, Laura Ovenden, Martin Galway and his colleagues at Herts for Learning, Bob Cox, Dylan Wiliam, friends and colleagues at Oxford University Press, Louise Johns-Shepherd and the team at the CLPE, Lesley Hendy, Jonathan Douglas and all at the National Literacy Trust and Mike Dodsworth, from whom I first heard the peach story (and who tells it far, far better than I ever will).

Giants one and all.

PART 1
Teaching by the book

Introduction

A case for books: putting literature at the heart of primary education

A story about peaches

Long ago and far away, a traveller was walking through a village when he came across an old man sat by the side of the road. Next to the old man was a great basket filled to the top with ripe peaches. The traveller stopped to watch as the man took a peach from the basket and bit into it. When he had finished, the old man licked his fingers clean and then carefully planted the peach stone in the sandy soil. Then he took another peach from the basket, ate it and again planted the stone.

The traveller watched this process continue for a few minutes before approaching the old man. 'Excuse me for interrupting, but I have a question. Why are you bothering to plant these peach stones? It will be many years before they grow into trees tall enough to bear fruit. You are an old man and you will not live long enough to enjoy their fruit.'

The old man smiled. 'You're right,' he said. 'But I'm not planting them for me. Just as my ancestors planted the trees that gave me these peaches, so the stones that I plant today will one day be covered in sweet fruit that will be enjoyed by those who come after me. I am planting them for my grandchildren and my grandchildren's grandchildren.' With that, the old man passed the traveller a peach.

The traveller ate his peach in silence. When he had finished, he bent down and carefully planted the stone in the soil.

Teaching English by the Book

Teaching English by the Book is based on a very simple idea: great books, wonderful poems and other rich texts should sit at the heart of the primary English curriculum.

Of course this sounds like an obvious idea. And yet, in many primary classrooms, the English curriculum has come to be organised in a different way. The pressures of the curriculum, national assessments and demands on time can lead to a model where reading, writing and grammar and punctuation are given separate slots on the timetable; a model where different aspects of English are taught as separate skills: grammar and punctuation knowledge here, answering ten comprehension questions about an extract there; a model where writing is taught through learning the features of different text types, separate from the books that children are reading in class.

It is unlikely that the curriculum has been planned in this way. Often the curriculum in schools grows organically and, over time, new features and initiatives are added to the overall body of what is taught. *Teaching English by the Book* will make a case for thinking about English as a connected whole, considering why and how a rich text can be the catalyst for teaching the many different facets of English.

While the chapters of the book consider each element of the English curriculum individually, the central message that runs through this book is that they are not discrete elements. Each facet of English that we teach depends on the others: spoken language makes reading and writing possible; an understanding of how English grammar works supports our comprehension; reading widely is crucial for effective writing. Where teaching uses great books to make links between them, each of these elements creates something greater than the sum of their parts. How these elements are weaved together will be different in every school, reflecting the beliefs of teachers and school leaders and the needs of the children the school serves. Rather than mandate one way of teaching English, this book seeks to share the key knowledge and ideas that will support a school to create a curriculum and model of teaching that are right for the school and its unique context.

A second message from *Teaching English by the Book* is that great English teaching is about more than just reading, writing, speaking and listening. These four aspects of the curriculum form *literacy*. Being literate is the very minimum we should expect from children when they leave primary school. Literacy is important, but it is just one part of the subject of *English*. As well as learning to read well and express themselves clearly through speech and writing, English teaching means giving children access to all the things we can learn from great books and stories. It gives them the chance to consider ideas beyond their own experience and encounter concepts that have never occurred to them before, to hear and read beautiful language and experience what it's like to lose themselves in a story, caught up in excitement, laughter, fear or joy.

The third key message in this book is that while we are teaching children to become accomplished readers and writers, to master the elements of reading and writing that are assessed in national tests, we should concentrate on some of the more-subtle aspects of English, too. The technical aspects of reading – decoding, understanding and responding – are vital but so is helping children to develop a genuine desire to read. Technical proficiency in writing, including a control of grammar and punctuation for effect, is necessary for success but so is children seeing themselves as writers, approaching writing like a crafts-man and measuring their words carefully to communicate exactly what they wish to their reader. There is a reciprocal relationship between technical skills and attitude in both reading and writing, and we can help children to develop their proficiency in English by encouraging both strands to flourish.

Another story about peaches

A rich text-based curriculum does more than help children to become better readers and writers. Sharing great books gives children the opportunity to encounter new language and new ideas, broadening their horizons and helping them to think about something in a different way. Books can transport children to new places and different times, allowing them to see through the eyes of others. Great texts give children a model for expressing themselves clearly in speech and writing, building an understanding of how language can be shaped for a particular purpose or audience.

Sometimes the effect of sharing a book is immediate. Perhaps a child takes an idea and it changes the way they see the world. Perhaps a word or phrase is borrowed and appears in a child's next piece of writing. Perhaps a book prompts a child to go and read another similar book, setting a chain of reading in motion. When this happens, it is wonderful.

But it is more likely that the benefits of a rich text-based curriculum will be more gradual, building slowly over time. As teachers, the language and ideas in books we share might not bear fruit until long after the children we teach have left our class.

When we share great literature with children, we are planting peach stones.

James Clements – March 2017

Choosing the right texts

Exploring the potential of great books

In the 2014 National Curriculum (DfE, 2013) progression in reading is driven by the challenge of the texts children read. There is no set of reading skills that grow steadily more challenging. Instead, the same broad skills and competencies are applied to texts that gradually increase in challenge.

Despite this, the teaching of reading in primary schools can sometimes focus on the discrete teaching of comprehension skills. This may be due to the lasting influence of the Primary Strategy and its assessment focuses, individually assessed and recorded using the Assessing Pupil Progress sheets (DfES, 2006). It may be the influence of published reading schemes that are built on ladders of reading skills. Or it could be a desire by schools and teachers to achieve well in the high-stakes national assessments by trying to make use of the Key Stage 2 test domains (originally created for test developers to ensure coverage of the National Curriculum) as a basis for teaching reading (DfE, 2016) in an effort to cover all of the elements that will be tested.

Whatever the reason, the teaching of reading (and writing) in the primary years is often broken down into a set of generic skills to be mastered. If children can learn to predict and infer, retrieve and record, then they will go on to become confident readers and writers. While research suggests that there are specific reading strategies that can be actively and consciously used to support comprehension (Palincsar and Brown, 1984), this is very different from basing all teaching on a set of generic comprehension skills that a reader draws on to make meaning from a text. Indeed, there is discussion about the value of basing the teaching of reading on these skills and whether they are transferable from book to book (Willingham and Lovette, 2014).

The fact is that reading and writing cannot be taught in a vacuum. Children need the opportunity to practise and develop as readers and writers by reading texts and being inspired to write by those texts.

And it matters which texts we choose to share with children.

Choosing 'the right text'

Choosing the right texts sits at the heart of an effective text-based curriculum. But who should do the choosing, by what criteria should they choose and what exactly makes 'the right text'?

The books children will read at school can be divided into different purposes depending on where in the curriculum they will be used, what they will be used to teach and who they will be read with. There will be books that children have chosen themselves and others that have been chosen by an adult. There will be texts that are being read purely for the pleasure they bring and others that have been selected to be studied in a particular area of the curriculum. The purpose of reading a text helps to define whether it is 'the right text'. The right text for teaching a Year 2 unit of work on letter writing will be very different from the right text for a Year 6 looking for something to read on the bus as they travel to school.

Of course this distinction between 'books to study' and 'books for enjoyment' is an artificial one. We would hope that there would be considerable overlap between the two. We want children to enjoy the books they study at school, finding them interesting, exciting or delightful. Equally, it is through children's own self-directed reading that they will develop into confident readers, putting in the reading miles that will develop their fluency and reading stamina, building their vocabulary and improving their general knowledge. However, it is useful to divide the purposes for selecting a book into these two crude categories when we are thinking about who should choose the text.

Books chosen by children and books chosen by adults

There is a strong case to be made that once a child can decode fluently, they should be given the freedom to read whatever they wish in their independent reading. Children benefit from the time and space to make their own choices and follow their own interests. Giving children access to a wide choice of texts and allowing them the time to read them are two of the easiest things we can do in schools to create confident readers. If that leads to children reading books that we as adults don't think of as being sufficiently good quality, then so be it. If it leads to a child reading every book in a long series or every book by a favourite author one after another, then that's fine too, even if it means that children reread a book that they love three times in a row or take on a book that's too tough-going (at the moment), before eventually giving up after three days. These are the things that mature readers do all the time. It is by choosing the books they wish to read (and getting that choice wrong sometimes) that children slowly become real readers. Of course we can advise children, recommending other books they may like to broaden their palate as a reader, but the importance of the texts that children *want* to read should never be underestimated. Research has shown the power of children having agency over the books that they read (Clark and Phythian-Sence, 2008).

But that doesn't mean that we should only make use of the books that children find instantly appealing. Quite the opposite. In schools we have a responsibility to broaden children's horizons by introducing them to the richest and most beautiful texts possible. Every child should have the opportunity to read and study both the great works of children's literature and also some of the wonderful fiction and non-fiction written for children today. Children should encounter books that perhaps they wouldn't choose to read themselves, books that they might struggle to access on their own and texts that introduce them to great ideas and language and take them beyond their current life experience. These books, the books children *study* as part of the curriculum, need to be carefully chosen to give them access to the very best books and language possible. For many children, if they aren't introduced to these rich texts at school, they won't ever meet them.

When thinking about selecting the right text in this chapter, we are thinking about texts that will be put to a purpose for a specific teaching or curriculum aim – the basis of a unit of work in English, a stimulus for writing or to read with a small group to develop comprehension. For children's independent reading for pleasure, we already know the right text: it's the one they want to read.

Choosing texts to study

So how can we choose the right texts to share at school? Is there even such a thing as 'the right text'? Three useful ways of thinking about texts the choice of texts are: potential, preference and challenge.

Potential

Tennant *et al.* (2016) use the term 'potential' to think about the qualities a particular book might offer for teaching. They suggest twelve aspects when thinking about a text:

- Subject – what is the text about?
- Text purpose and intended readership – is it written to amuse, persuade, inform, warn? Is it a balanced view?
- Theme – the deeper meaning
- Narrative features – from whose perspective is it written? Where is it set?
- Literary features – particular stylistic devices
- Language features
- Grammar, syntax, sentence structure
- Vocabulary
- Historical, social and cultural context – where is it set and who is represented?

- Coherence
- Visual features – design of material
- Making links to background knowledge

Tennant *et al.* (2016)

Assessing a text for its potential relies on familiarity with the text and matching it to the intended teaching and learning outcomes. The ability to do this comes from knowing the texts well enough to know how they might be used as illustrations or stimuli for a particular area of the curriculum. One potential barrier to this is it requires teachers having a sufficiently wide knowledge of children's literature. Research from Cremin *et al.* (2009) suggests that as a body of professionals, teachers' knowledge of literature can be lacking. Many of the teachers interviewed for the project didn't know where to go to find out about quality literature, nor did they have the time to read and keep abreast of children's books. This is not surprising considering many primary teachers are not English specialists. For a text-based curriculum to be successful, the teachers who are experts in children's literature at a school need an opportunity to share their expertise and those who are not will need support to find the right books and make the best use of them. Staff book clubs, the sharing of resources for finding books such as those on p. 17, and the type of structured but flexible text-based curriculum outlined in Chapters 3 and 4 can all help to address this, but none of these are substitutes for teachers carving out the time to engage with children's literature. The best teachers of reading are teachers who read, and that means teachers finding time to stay up-to-date and engage with children's literature.

Preference

Every teacher is likely to have their own favourite children's books. These might be new books that they have discovered and are excited about teaching or they might be books from their childhood, books they used when they were training, books they have read with their own children or books that they've had success teaching with in the past. Sometimes the fact that a book is an exciting new purchase or a trusty old favourite is reason enough to choose it to share with children.

A good English curriculum should allow teachers some choice in the books they share and space for them to talk with excitement about the ones they love. Hopefully that enthusiasm will be infectious and that is what we need if we are going to help a generation of children become lifelong readers. This might mean occasionally sharing a book that would be seen as being too easy for a particular year group. This shouldn't matter sometimes – Year 4 will take plenty from of an enthusiastic reading of *Would You Rather . . .* by John Burningham with the chance to talk about their choices. Equally, if the text seems very challenging, a good teacher can scaffold and support children to understand it and take something from the text.

Challenge

If we want children to grow to become confident readers, we can help them by choosing challenging texts to study.

Assessing the challenge that a text presents isn't the straightforward concept that it might appear. There is more to the level of challenge than the number of pages and size of font. Indeed, it has been suggested that some methods of quantifying the challenge of a book in these terms can present both conceptual and technical difficulties, masking the true accessibility of a book (Lemov *et al.*, 2016).

There are many types of challenge a text can bring and the challenge of each will be unique to each reader, depending on the existing body of knowledge they bring to a text. The more that a child knows about a particular subject, the easier it is for them to make sense of the words on the page, adding them to their existing schema (their framework of the world). A child's background knowledge aside, when we're thinking about teaching, there are two main challenges we need to be aware of:

Language – there are several ways that language can make a text challenging. The first is vocabulary, the words themselves. It might be the technical language in a non-fiction book about space – *nebulae* or *parsec*, or unfamiliar words in a classic text – *apoplexy* or *buccaneering* in Robert Louis Stevenson's *Treasure Island*. Clearly, understanding these words is a key factor in understanding the text. The second way text can be challenging is through the structure of the language – the syntax and grammar. Complex sentences with numerous embedded clauses can present a challenge to understanding. *Alice's Adventures in Wonderland*, for example, begins with a multi-clause sentence that is 57 words long and can stretch the understanding of the most confident reader. Another potential challenge is the register of the text, the style of language, grammar and words used in a particular situation. If the register is very formal, as in some older texts, or uses a local dialect, such as Alan Garner's *The Weirdstone of Brisingamen*, this can also provide a barrier to understanding for some readers.

Ideas – it isn't always the language that can be a barrier to understanding in a challenging text: it might be the ideas it introduces too. The book might be set in an unfamiliar place or time; it might feature complex characters or situations that require empathy to understand. The text might introduce children to new concepts or complicated ideas, taking them beyond their current life experience.

Unfamiliar vocabulary and language structures and complicated ideas can all provide challenges to a reader, but they are also reasons why we should read and share these books with children.

Challenge doesn't just come from the text itself; it is also what we do with it that matters. A unit of work might be based on a seemingly simple text but lead to very rich piece of writing – an extended narrative based on the almost wordless picturebook *Mr Wuffles* by David Weisner, for example. Conversely, with careful scaffolding, a challenging text can be accessed by even young children. Selecting a text that is rich enough in language and ideas to challenge every child is important. It is easier to support a child to understand a text than it is to manufacture challenge when it just isn't there.

Think and reflect

Beautiful non-fiction

In the modern world, if we need to find information we tend to go online to find what we wish to know quickly and easily. This is a very different experience from browsing a non-fiction book – in some ways much easier but in others a less-rich experience. Rather than the internet spelling the end of children's non-fiction, these books are going through a renaissance, with rich non-fiction texts that are both fascinating and beautiful. Here are some glorious non-fiction texts:

Star Stuff by Stephanie Roth Sisson

The Number Devil by Hans Magnus Enzenberger

The Wonder Garden by Kristina S. Williams and Jenny Broom

The Man Who Walked between the Towers by Mordecai Gerstein

You Are Stardust by Elin Kelsey and Soyeon Kim

Mythological Monsters of Ancient Greece by Sara Fanelli

Exotic Animals A–Z by Marc Martin

Fantastically Great Women Who Changed the World by Kate Pankhurst

Enormous Smallness by Matthew Burgess

Literary heritage texts

Sometimes the term 'challenging texts' is conflated with literary heritage texts, 'famous writings from the past which still influence the present' (Cox, 2014). There's no reason why a challenging text should be a classic work of literature: many contemporary children's books are rich and challenging, but literary heritage texts are important part of a text-based curriculum.

Literary heritage texts can provide a specific challenge linked to both language and ideas. Many classic texts not only employ archaic vocabulary but syntactical structures that may be challenging for children. After two opening sentences of 57 and 55 words respectively, *Alice's Adventures in Wonderland* launches into this 141-word sentence:

> There was nothing so *very* remarkable in that; nor did Alice think it so *very* much out of the way to hear the Rabbit say to itself, 'Oh dear! Oh dear! I shall be late!' (when she thought it over afterwards, it occurred to her that she ought to have wondered at this, but at the time it all seemed quite natural); but when the Rabbit actually *took a watch out of its waistcoat-pocket*, and looked at it, and then hurried on, Alice started to her feet, for it flashed across her mind that she had never before seen a rabbit with either a waistcoat-pocket, or a watch to take out of it, and burning with curiosity, she ran across the field after it, and fortunately was just in time to see it pop down a large rabbit-hole under the hedge.

This is a challenge to follow even if you know the meaning of each of the individual words. Despite their potential difficulty, literary heritage texts remain valuable to teach, partly because many texts studied at secondary school and later fall into this category. If children are suddenly exposed to a very challenging text for the first time at the age of 11, it won't be surprising if they struggle to make sense of it and don't enjoy the experience. Suddenly being asked to study a Shakespeare play or a piece of classic poetry will be difficult if the children haven't experienced anything like them before. If we can introduce children to them in primary school, before their attitudes harden and their minds close, we will be doing them a great service. Alongside being confident readers, if we can help children to be excited, enthusiastic and fearless when confronted with challenging literature, and if they can carry this attitude to their secondary school English lessons, there's a good chance they'll go on to successfully access the secondary curriculum.

The benefits of introducing primary children to great texts from the past go beyond giving them practice for secondary school, however. Primary education is about more than preparation for secondary school.

These books can be hugely beneficial for their reading and use of spoken and written English, letting them see how authors use language to communicate complex ideas and rich themes. Another reason to share classic texts with children is cultural capital. Many great works of literature have a cultural resonance beyond the books themselves, and readers meet the ideas, narrative structures and characters again and again in other books, in films and on television. Giving children access to these stories gives them access to the world of literature later on. First and foremost, many literary heritage texts are great stories. Fairy tales, myths and legends from across the world and great novels and poems are constantly being retold and adapted today, often hundreds of years after they were first told. The reason we retell them is that they're engaging and exciting, wise and wonderful. And that's a very good reason to ensure they are represented on a text-based curriculum.

Whether contemporary or classic, for many children studying challenging texts is enjoyable. Having to think hard about something is a sign that learning is happening. Every child should have the opportunity to experience the sense of achievement that comes when the seemingly incomprehensible suddenly swims into focus. At the heart of this approach is helping children to identify themselves as scholars, as the sort of people who take on and understand challenging books. If children are only ever confronted with texts that are immediately accessible, chosen because they are relevant to their current interests, they are denied this opportunity. If we want our children to become lifelong readers, we need to teach everyone to read to a good standard *and* give them the opportunity to think and talk and argue about great books and the complex ideas they contain.

Why not try?

It can be difficult trying to find great books and keep abreast of the many wonderful books for children that are published each year. Some suggestions for inspiration might come from:

(continued)

Why not try? (*continued*)

Shakespeare and More booklists – a collection of high-quality books selected by teachers across the UK: www.shakespeare andmore.com/greatbooks

Centre for Literacy in Education Core Books – a selection of high-quality texts: www.clpe.org.uk/corebooks

Just Imagine Story Centre – support with finding books for a particular setting, age group or purpose: www.justimagine storycentre.co.uk

Book competitions and awards – the longlists for children's book awards can be a great source of new books. Try the Carnegie and the Greenaway Awards: www.carnegiegreenaway.org.uk

For a comprehensive guide to children's literature and the types of text that can be useful in the classroom and be enjoyed by teachers and children alike (and some wonderful reading lists) see Nikki Gamble's *Exploring Children's Literature* (2013).

In the next chapter we'll consider how this wide range of books selected carefully for reasons of purpose, potential, preference, and challenge can be organised into a rich text-based curriculum.

In summary

- Becoming a confident reader and writer is about more than mastering a set of discrete skills
- The choice of texts we use to teach English matters a great deal – both to introduce them to texts they might not

(*continued*)

> ## In summary (*continued*)
>
> encounter otherwise and as a rich model for their own language development
> - Texts that are going to be studied in English lessons might be chosen by the teacher for reasons of potential, preference and challenge
> - A text-based curriculum draws on a wide range of texts, including literary heritage books and contemporary literature

Bibliography

Clark, C. and Phythian-Sence, C. (2008) *Interesting Choice: The (Relative) Importance of Choice and Interest in Reader Engagement*. London: National Literacy Trust.

Cox, B. (2014) *Opening Doors to Famous Poetry and Prose: Ideas and Resources for Accessing Literary Heritage Works*. Carmarthen: Crown House.

Cremin, T., Mottram, M., Collins, F., Powell, S. and Safford, K. (2009) Teachers as readers: building communities of readers. *Literary*, 43 (1), 11–19.

DfE (2013) *National Curriculum in England: Primary Curriculum*. London: DfE.

DfE (2016) *English Reading Test Framework: National Curriculum Tests from 2016 for Test Developers*. London: DfE.

DfES (2006) *Primary National Strategy – A Framework for Literacy*. London: DfES.

Gamble, N. (2013) *Exploring Children's Literature*. London: SAGE.

Lemov, D., Driggs, C. and Woolway, E. (2016) *Reading Reconsidered: A Practical Guide to Rigorous Literacy Instruction*. San Francisco: Jossey-Bass.

Palincsar, A. S. and Brown, A. L. (1984) Reciprocal teaching of comprehension-fostering and comprehension-monitoring activities. *Cognition and Instruction*, 1 (2), 117–175.

Tennant, W., Reedy, D., Hobsbaum, A. and Gamble, N. (2016) *Guiding Readers: Layers of Meaning*. London: UCL, Institute of Education.

Willingham, D. T. and Lovette, G. (2014) *Can Reading Comprehension Be Taught? Teachers College Record*. New York: NCR.

Literature

Alice's Adventures in Wonderland by Lewis Carroll
Mr Wuffles by David Weisner
The Weirdstone of Brisingamen by Alan Garner
Treasure Island by Robert Louis Stevenson
Would You Rather . . . by John Burningham

The English curriculum

Planning for meaningful learning

Many schools in the UK and further afield are now exploring the benefits of a text-based approach to English teaching, with rich books, poems and plays sitting at the heart of the curriculum. This chapter will explore how a school may go about creating a text-based curriculum, making use of the breadth of the curriculum to help children to become confident and keen users of English.

A curriculum of one's own

A school's curriculum is more than just what should be taught to children. It also encompasses how the learning will be organised and any other experiences that will be planned for children. Wiliam (2013) outlines three levels for the curriculum:

1. **The intended curriculum** – the curriculum as prescribed by a national curriculum: the specified topics, ideas and content that children should be taught
2. **The implemented curriculum** – the schemes of work, lesson plans and taught content
3. **The enacted curriculum** – how the planned units of work or schemes are implemented in the classroom

This chapter will concentrate on the first two curriculum areas: what is to be taught and how this might be organised to create meaningful learning experiences for children.

The structure and organisation of a particular school's curriculum will reflect the demands of the national curriculum and any national assessments, the needs of the pupils at the school and the beliefs and ethos of the school's teachers and leaders. A successful curriculum needs to be unique to each individual school and there is unlikely to be an existing model for an English curriculum that can be purchased or downloaded from the internet and align with the school's needs perfectly. While different schools will (and should) settle on very different curriculum models, it is likely that all schools will need to consider some fundamental ideas and principles when developing a curriculum. These principles will then inform the planning of the curriculum to ensure that it is purposeful and effective.

Purpose and planning

The first step in planning the curriculum is to decide on its purpose. What does the curriculum hope to achieve? The different purposes may reflect beliefs held by the school leaders. They may also need to reflect the demands of a national curriculum or national assessment. These principles might be driven by the desire for every child to:

- Develop strong speaking and listening skills that allow them to express themselves, communicating confidently across a range of appropriately challenging contexts
- Read fluently and understand a wide range of texts appropriate for a child of their age
- Choose to read widely and often in their own time
- Produce independent writing that is both technically proficient and creative, tailored to the demands of purpose and audience

These principles or others like them give a clear end point to aim for, but the challenge is how this can be translated into a rich English curriculum. One way to consider the English curriculum is to think of it as a set of vehicles that can be used to help children to develop key knowledge, skills and characteristics that will help them to successfully meet their aims. When considering the vehicles available to teach English in school, the list might look something like this:

- English lessons
- Small-group reading
- Shared reading
- Independent reading
- Reading aloud
- Phonics sessions
- Shared writing
- Guided writing
- Discrete grammar and punctuation teaching
- Cross-curricular links to English

An important factor in the success of an effective curriculum is for these individual elements to work together. This may mean that they teach different aspects of English, sometimes as discrete entities and some-times working together.

Small-group reading

Small-group reading comes in many forms, but can be defined by an adult working with a small group of children, using a text to teach reading. This may be the familiar model of guided reading, where the group are organised by current reading attainment and the text is closely matched to the group's needs, or it may take another form, such as a literature circle or book group.

Small-group reading can be hugely valuable due to the interactive nature of a group in which children can discuss ideas and learn from their peers and the teacher. The small group enables the teacher to focus on each individual child, targeting their questioning and addressing any misconceptions as they occur – something that can be difficult when working with the whole class. It also allows the teacher to assess the children's reading skills without having to resort to written tests, which are often as much a test of writing ability as they are of reading.

The principle challenge for this type of teaching is ensuring that the children who are not working with an adult are engaged in meaningful learning or consolidation rather than filler activities. Care also needs to be taken in planning so that children who are not yet reading texts that are at an age-appropriate level make the necessary progress so that they are able to catch up with their peers.

Think and reflect

When planning small-group reading, either in class or across a school, it is important to remember that it is flexible and can be structured however the teacher or subject leader sees fit.

In traditional guided reading it is not uncommon to find children organised into five groups of six, each using a levelled text. They read with the teacher for 20 or 30 minutes once a week, while the other children move around a carousel of activities. If this is the best way to organise small group reading for every classroom, then that is fine. But if it happens that way because that is the orthodoxy, then, clearly, that is not fine. Every part of the curriculum has to earn its place and be as effective as it can be.

Grouping children – children should be grouped together for sound educational reasons. That might be because of the level of challenge offered by a text (linked to potential, preference and challenge – see Chapter 1) or it might be that they share a particular need (an aspect of decoding or comprehension). But groups can be organised for other reasons, too – by interest or as mixed-ability to give children the opportunity to learn from one another. Some schools have employed a model where guided reading groups are slightly mismatched, with children moving regularly between groups.

(continued)

Think and reflect (*continued*)

On occasion children have the opportunity to be the expert in a group, modelling to other children, while on other occasions they have the opportunity to work with stronger readers who can provide a model for fluency. Groups do not need to be of consistent size either: some children may benefit from smaller groups for an intensive focus on a particular aspect of reading or larger groups for more time to spend discussing the text.

Frequency and length of sessions – group reading doesn't need to happen daily for 20 minutes: sessions could be longer or happen less frequently, depending on what is being taught. For some children who especially need it a weekly session with the teacher might not be enough; those who are struggling with reading will still benefit from as much time reading with the teacher as possible.

The carousel of activities – there is no set structure for organising small-group reading sessions. While a carousel *can* work well, it can also be time-consuming to plan and organise and it can be difficult to ensure that all activities are meaningful and develop some aspect of children's reading. Once children are fluent readers, the most useful activity might be simply reading independently.

Shared reading

Shared reading (sometimes organised as whole-class guided reading) is where the whole class reads the same text together. Shared reading may happen as part of an English lesson or in its own space on the curriculum. The teacher could read aloud or individual children could take it in turns to read. Before, during and after reading, the whole class takes part in a discussion about the text, giving children the chance to hear different opinions and interpretations of what they have read. Afterwards, the whole class might undertake the same follow-up tasks or there might be different tasks for different children, depending on the support they need to become stronger readers or users of English.

There are a number of benefits to a shared-reading approach. Every child reads and/or listens to the same texts, which might not happen in small-group reading, where texts are often matched to children's current reading level. Shared reading ensures entitlement – every child is able to study and enjoy the same challenging texts.

The challenge for effective shared reading is ensuring that every child can access the text. This relies on skilful scaffolding by the teacher – helping all children to access the text whether through reading aloud to ensure children's developing decoding skills don't prevent understanding or through careful pre-teaching and questioning to support children to access a challenging text. Chapter 5 outlines some practical approaches that can be used in shared reading.

Independent reading

Independent reading is the reading that children do in their own time, away from formal teaching situations. This may be reading that happens at home or at school.

Independent reading time is where children have the opportunity to read for sustained periods of time, building their fluency and reading stamina. It also gives children an opportunity to enjoy reading with no other purpose than for the reading itself. For many children, reading will be a regular occurrence at home, but for some, independent reading will only happen regularly at school. If these children do not have time to read independently at school, they simply will not get this valuable experience.

Think and reflect

Choosing texts for independent reading

The texts that children read in independent reading vary widely from school to school, and this can generate strong debate.

(continued)

Think and reflect (*continued*)

In some schools children read books chosen for them by an adult. In others they have a choice of texts drawn from a collection of levelled or 'suitable' texts. In other schools children are afforded a completely free choice of book.

Those who advocate the use of levelled books or adults supporting children's choices make the valid argument about whether time spent reading books at a level too easy or too challenging is time wasted. There are only so many hours to read, so shouldn't children be reading a text matched closely to their current level of reading development? After all, this is what is going to help them develop fluency as a reader. For children in the early stages of learning to read, this is certainly true, as a child may select a book which they are simply unable to read.

However, another equally convincing argument can be made for children having autonomy over the books that they read, especially considering the motivational power of a child choosing their own reading material. As adults, we often enjoy reading a text that we don't find particularly challenging – a book on holiday or a magazine, perhaps. We also sometimes take on a challenging read – a technical text linked to work, a piece of literary fiction or a classic text. Shouldn't children also have these reading experiences – the opportunity to find a book challenging and labour on with it, the opportunity to give up and try something different or the opportunity to reread an old favourite, just as mature readers do? Of course the counter-argument says that children *aren't* mature readers yet . . .

Having considered this debate:

- What are *your* thoughts on the books that children read independently?
- How do your beliefs affect the organisation of independent reading in your school or classroom?

Reading aloud

While reading aloud is a regular feature of Early Years and Key Stage 1 classrooms, opportunities to listen to and enjoy books can decrease as children move through the school. Listening to a book being read aloud should form an important part of the reading curriculum throughout a school. Reading aloud supports the development of children's vocabulary and their background knowledge, key aspects of becoming confident readers and writers. This is especially important for children who don't read widely in their own time or might not be lucky enough to have someone who reads to them at home. It can also be an opportunity for a teacher to model the process of comprehension, pausing occasionally to show children how a reader makes sense of text that is at first challenging or inaccessible. It is also a way of developing children's reading palates, introducing them to texts and authors that they might not choose themselves. Listening to a book being read aloud by a skilled reader allows a child to hear what fluent reading sounds like, listening to the different prosodic elements such as intonation, pauses and where the stress is placed in different words. In addition, listening to an engaging story or a fascinating non-fiction book can help to show children that reading can be an enjoyable activity, supporting their positive attitude to reading.

The challenge with reading aloud is finding time for an activity that can seem frivolous in a busy curriculum and which doesn't lend itself to a clear and measurable learning objective.

Phonics sessions

The 2014 National Curriculum (DfE, 2013) emphasises the use of synthetic phonics in the teaching of reading to children at the start of school. In most English schools, phonics sessions are discrete teaching sessions, often using a published scheme of work to systematically teach children to word-read accurately and fluently. This follows the findings of the Rose Review (2006) that suggests:

> High-quality, systematic phonic work as defined by the review should be taught discretely. The knowledge, skills and understanding that

constitute high-quality phonic work should be taught as the prime approach in learning to decode (to read) and encode (to write/spell) print.

McGuinness (2004) suggests a number of features shared by an effective phonics programme:

- No sight words (except high-frequency words with rare spellings)
- No letter names
- Sound-to-print orientation: phonemes, not letters, are the basis for the code
- Teach phonemes only – no other sound units
- Begin with basic code (a one-to-one correspondence between 40 phonemes and their most common spelling)
- Teach children to identify and sequence sounds in real words by segmenting and blending using letters
- Teach children how to write each letter
- Integrate writing into every lesson
- Link writing (spelling) and reading to ensure children learn the alphabet is a code and that codes are reversible: encoding/decoding
- Spelling should be accurate or, at a minimum, phonetically accurate (all things within reason)
- Lessons should move on to include the advanced spelling code (the 136 remaining, common spellings)

This explicit teaching of phonics will be time-limited: once children can decode accurately, they can use their reading skills to independently access the rich and motivating texts that are advocated in this book. Fluent word-reading allows children to read whichever book they choose, opening up a world of rich and wonderful books to them.

Specific phonics sessions are unlikely to be the only place for children to develop their decoding skills. As the Rose Review notes:

The best practice also took advantage of opportunities . . . [for] children to apply their developing decoding and encoding skills to the reading and writing of fiction and non-fiction in work across the curriculum. This interplay of phonic work within the wider curriculum was a strong feature of good teaching: it helped children to see the purpose of phonic work as they reinforced their developing skills by applying them to worthwhile and interesting curricular content.

(Rose, 2006)

If we want children to become confident readers as quickly as possible, then it is likely that they will benefit from a systematic approach to learning how the alphabetic code of English works and plenty of opportunities to use and apply this knowledge. It is also vital that discrete phonics teaching takes place within a rich text-based curriculum. While children are learning to word-read, they will continue to listen to and enjoy a wide range of books and stories that are read to them, with teachers making use of the other vehicles across the reading curriculum to share wonderful texts.

Shared writing

Shared writing allows a teacher to model the thought process involved in writing, demonstrating how a writer makes important decisions about the words and phrases they use and how they organise them. In shared writing the teacher and class compose a piece of writing together, with everyone contributing their thoughts and ideas to the process. At its most effective, the teacher is doing more than simply acting as a scribe: they are leading the writing, showing the children how a writer works as a craftsman and shaping words and phrases in order to communicate a specific idea or create a particular effect.

Teachers can help children to consider the qualities that make one word, phrase or grammatical construction better suited to the context than another by thinking aloud as they write. A teacher modelling writing to the class might say something like this as she writes:

'Sara ran home.' Ok, well, 'ran' is fine, but 'rushed' might be better as it creates a sense of urgency. She's not just running for the fun of it: there's a reason. Hmm, now how can I show that she's upset? I could just write that, but perhaps I could make the reader do some work and show that she's sad instead. What about an adverbial clause at the start? How about, 'Crying,'? Hmm, how about something stronger? 'Sobbing, Sara rushed home.' What about describing it instead? 'With tears streaming down her face, Sara rushed home.' That's better; I'll come back to it later to see how it flows into the next sentence.

Thinking aloud like this shows children a writer's thought process. It enables children to appreciate the merits of different vocabulary choices, structural features or literary devices, and, over time, children will learn to make use of these in their own writing.

In successful shared writing the children are aware of the audience and purpose of the text being created so they can think about how these affect the text. It is important that the teacher doesn't simply model the initial writing but also the drafting process, showing the children how writers make changes to their work as they write and, afterwards, reading it back to them.

Managing classroom talk in shared writing can be challenging, ensuring all children are actively engaged with the writing process and everyone is thinking and making suggestions. This might be approached through paired talk or the use of notes or individual whiteboards.

Guided writing

Guided writing works best when the teacher works with a small group of children, focusing on a specific element of writing. The children don't necessarily need to be working at a similar level; they might simply have a shared need or focus. The time might be used for direct teaching, with the group then practising what they've learnt, or the children could work on their own pieces of writing, with the teacher on hand to offer targeted support as they write. The group nature of guided writing means that children can discuss ideas and learn from their peers. The small group gives the teacher the chance to check children's understanding and address any misconceptions they may have, something that can be difficult when working with the whole class.

In successful guided writing each session is based on previous assessment: through the marking of written work or ongoing assessments, the teacher has identified an aspect of writing that would benefit from focused teaching. The session is planned around areas of development for specific pupils. While the teacher supports children to improve their writing, focusing on specific elements, including content and ideas, structural features, language and grammatical features, spelling and presentation, the emphasis should always be on the intended audience and purpose of the piece and how these elements contribute to effective communication.

Discrete grammar, punctuation and spelling teaching

Research suggests that discrete teaching of the English-language elements of the curriculum are of limited benefit to children's writing (Jones *et al.*, 2013). However, due to national assessments and a curriculum that places emphasis on the technical aspects of language, many schools will teach key elements of the curriculum discretely. Chapter 10 covers the teaching of grammar and punctuation in detail, but it is likely that the most effective English-language teaching feeds back into children's reading and writing. The aim of sessions is to improve children's understanding and control of English rather than to learn a body of specific knowledge in a vacuum.

Cross-curricular links

Reading and writing in subjects other than English can provide an excellent opportunity for children to develop their use of English.

Reading and writing for a purpose can be motivating and it provides an opportunity for children to put into practice what they have learnt through the English curriculum. Reading in other curriculum areas can also help with children's vocabulary development and background knowledge, giving them access to new words and ideas. Care needs to be taken that books are selected for reasons of potential, preference and challenge, rather than because they happen to match a curriculum topic in a subject like geography or history.

Think and reflect

In a rich text-based curriculum for English all children should have access to the same high-quality texts, with a skilled teacher supporting each child's understanding through questioning, targeted teaching and careful explanation. If the curriculum and teaching are working well, almost all children should have the opportunity to meet the age-related expectations for the curriculum that they are studying. In your school or classroom:

- Do all children have access to rich texts, even if they cannot yet read them independently?
- If children are not ready to access age-appropriate texts, what steps are taken to close this gap as quickly as possible?

Of course, there is no one model for a successful English curriculum. What is vital, however, is that each element has a clear rationale and that it has been carefully planned to ensure it is as effective as it can be in developing children's spoken language, reading, writing or positive attitudes to English. In the next chapter we will look in depth at the principal vehicle for English teaching: English lessons.

In summary

- An effective English curriculum requires careful planning and is built around key purposes identified by the school itself
- There are many different vehicles for teaching different aspects of English to children and these should work together to complement and support one another
- These curriculum vehicles might look very different from school to school, depending on the purpose
- Over the course of the curriculum, children should have access to a wide range of reading experiences: learning to decode fluently, talking and discussing books, developing their comprehension with challenging texts and being given the opportunity to reread to build fluency
- The curriculum needs to be planned so that children have access to many different books and texts: encountering rich and challenging texts, rereading old favourites and having the chance to choose their own books, sometimes getting the choice right and sometimes wrong

Bibliography

DfE (2013) *National Curriculum in England: Primary Curriculum*. London: DfE.

Jones, S. M., Myhill, D. A. and Bailey, T. C. (2013) Grammar for writing? An investigation into the effect of contextualised grammar teaching on student writing. *Reading and Writing*, 26 (8), 1241–1263.

McGuinness, D. (2004) *Early Reading Instruction: What Science Really Tells Us About How to Teach Reading*. Cambridge, MA: The MIT Press.

Rose, J. (2006) *Independent Review of the Teaching of Early Reading*. Nottingham: DfE.

Wiliam, D. (2013) *Redesigning Schooling: Principled Curriculum Design*. London: SSAT.

English lessons

Creating rich units of work

While rich English teaching will make use of all of the curriculum vehicles available, it is in English lessons where there is a sustained opportunity to bring together the different elements of English. This chapter will consider how a school might practically implement a text-based approach to teaching English.

Once we've chosen a rich text packed with potential and matched it to a place in the curriculum, the next step is to plan a unit of work based on it. This chapter will begin with the top level of curriculum planning – the intended curriculum – before addressing the level of a teacher's planning – the implemented curriculum – focusing on the features of an effective text-based unit.

A curriculum map for English lessons

Appendix I gives a suggested map for a text-based curriculum, outlining the books that could form the basis of a school's curriculum. (Editable versions can be downloaded for free from www.shakespeareandmore. com/unitplans.) When designing a text-based curriculum, schools will need to make decisions that reflect their own context and the needs of their children, so this model wouldn't be a perfect match for every school. However, it provides a useful model to explore the decisions and factors a school would need to consider when consolidating its own curriculum.

Coverage

Coverage is the enemy of good learning. If teachers have a curriculum to deliver with a set amount of content to cover over a certain number of weeks, that leaves little room for flexibility when things don't go as expected.

The curriculum model in Appendix I covers 32 weeks, allowing a primary school teacher 7 weeks of flexible time. They have space to teach something again the next day if the children didn't understand or the time to spend another few days on something if it's going especially well and the children would benefit from exploring something in greater depth or producing another piece of writing based on the text. When planning a text-based curriculum schools need to be careful not to pack so much in that teaching becomes about ticking things off as covered, rather than about the genuine (and often slightly messy) process of learning. Allowing some spare time in an English curriculum gives space for the realities that come with teaching in the classroom.

Prescription of texts to be studied

Deciding how prescriptive to be with the texts that are studied can be a challenge when planning a text-based curriculum. If the texts to be studied are chosen and allocated to different year groups centrally, it allows for progression and ensures that the texts studies will be chosen with a clear rationale. While it supports consistency and a clear progression in the books children are studying, this level of control can be counter-productive to good teaching. If a teacher is a confident teacher of English, they may have particular books that they wish to teach: preference is a legitimate reason for choosing to teach a book. Allocating texts centrally might mean opportunities are lost as teachers *have* to teach books, even though they may be reluctant to do so.

The opposite scenario is where teachers are given a completely free choice in the texts that they use in English lessons. But here we have the possibility of children studying the same 'old favourites' in multiple year groups as they travel through the school. And for teachers who

Table 3.1 Text-based units of work

Classic tales	These are texts that children *should* have the opportunity to study at school and that carry a cultural resonance – they are great stories in their own right, but they are also important because they are referenced in so many other stories. They are sometimes referred to as 'literary heritage texts'. They might be the original stories or high-quality retellings of them. For younger children this means learning about nursery rhymes and fairy stories; for older children a wide range of myths and legends from across the world, some stories from Shakespeare and other stories such as Robin Hood or tales of King Arthur and his knights.
Well-loved stories	These units introduce children to great works of children's literature that they should have the opportunity to read and enjoy. This ranges from classic picture books such as *Not Now Bernard* and *Dogger* to classics such as *Charlotte's Web* and *The Iron Man*. These are the books that no child should reach the age of 11 without having read.
Contemporary fiction	These units introduce children (and teachers) to some of the wonderful, rich contemporary fiction that is written for children today. These units are updated regularly, but provide teachers with books that they might not encounter otherwise if they are not readers of children's literature. This ranges from picture books for younger children such as *Oi Frog!* and for older children, such as *The Enemy* to novels such as *Rooftoppers* or *Railhead*.
Texts to inform	These units give children the opportunity to read, study and write texts to inform, including non-fiction books and websites.
Biography	Opportunities for biography writing are embedded within the text-based units, but are also a standalone unit linked to the wider curriculum.
Journalistic writing	Journalistic writing is often based on rich texts, but it can also be standalone units linked to real events. Journalistic units might be written as newspaper articles, magazine articles or film and online texts. In older year groups children consider biases in newspapers.
Poetry	Poetry is well-represented on the curriculum. Units of work give children the chance to read and respond to a wide range of different poetry and to learn and perform different poems. Children also have the opportunity to write poetry.

Table 3.1 Text-based units of work

Persuasive writing	Writing to persuade is an outcome for many text-based units, but is also a standalone unit linked to the wider curriculum.
Recounts	Recounts sit separately from the school's text-based curriculum. Instead, children write a recount of any educational visits they make or of any exciting events or visitors to school, giving them a real and meaningful experience to write about.

aren't confident in this area or who don't have the knowledge of children's literature needed to choose great texts to drive the curriculum, having some suggested texts can be very helpful.

The model in Appendix I uses a hybrid model of these two approaches. The year is divided into text-based units and, for each, a short selection of suitable texts is given. Teachers have the freedom to choose any of these texts, selecting the one that best captures their imagination. If a teacher has a better idea for a text to drive a particular unit, they can go and find the English subject leader and check that their proposed book isn't being taught elsewhere in the school and then use that instead. Because only 32 weeks of the curriculum are planned, there are likely to also be some spare weeks for each teacher to share the texts that they have particular enthusiasm for. Table 3.1 gives an overview of the different units across the school and the reason for studying each. The same units are studied more than once each year and across different year groups to allow children to return to the same ideas and types of text, building a deeper understanding.

Outcomes: products and purposes

For each text-based unit different outcomes are suggested. These are only suggestions and teachers have the freedom to deviate from these if they wish. Each unit has one or more suggested written outcome: these are not linked to specific text types or genres, but instead to the primary purpose for creating them: writing to entertain, describe, inform, instruct or persuade. The specific form of the writing will be linked to its purpose, but it is made clear that there will be some overlap within these purposes – an advert for a new theme park might be written to persuade, but it might also wish to entertain the reader; a non-fiction text about deforestation might seek to inform, but it could also be persuading the reader about the importance of the issue. In addition to written outcomes, the plan also suggests other outcomes – debates, presentations, performances etc. It is important to remember that a unit of work needn't always build to a piece of writing.

Grammar and punctuation

In the light of the 2014 National Curriculum (DfE, 2013) and the assessment model that accompanies it, the transcription elements of English – control over grammar, punctuation, handwriting and spelling – have become an increased focus for teachers in English schools. Opportunities for teaching grammar and punctuation drawn from the texts studied and the writing opportunities have been mapped onto the units. This gives children the opportunity to see how different language features work to create a specific effect. This is addressed in greater detail in Chapter 10.

A curriculum map like this provides a basis for the next stage of planning: devising individual units of work, each with a rich text sitting at the heart.

Planning a unit of work for English

There are many different ways of organising a text-based unit of work for English and each will depend on the teacher and their preferences, on the needs of the children in the class and on the specific opportunities that a particular book offers. When planning a text-based unit there are a number of considerations.

Duration of units and 'sketch planning'

A unit of work might last anywhere from a few days to a full half term. The duration depends on the text and the opportunities a teacher has planned from it. Generally, the younger a class are or the shorter a text is, the shorter the unit will be. However, by using several shorter texts together (for example, collecting a number of poems about nature or several picturebook versions of the same traditional tale), units composed of short texts can last longer. Some short texts might be the catalyst for a sustained unit of work – a particularly rich picture book such as *Night of the Gargoyles* by Eve Bunting or *The Island* by Armin Greder might form the basis of a substantial unit. As always, the needs of the children and the potential of the book are our guide.

What is important, whatever the length of the unit, is to think about the unit as one coherent plan, rather than three or four individual weeks of learning joined together. The cycle of weekly planning can make this difficult, with the unit planned in detail five days ahead. This means planning for Friday before Monday to Thursday have been taught. Many teachers find themselves planning at the start of a week and then spending the rest of the week changing their plans and making alterations in light of what has actually happened in their lessons. A better model, where the whole unit is seen as a coherent whole, building to a particular purpose *and* where time isn't wasted planning in detail something that actually doesn't happen, is *sketch planning*.

Sketch planning

This model of *sketch planning* is key to the success of an extended text-based unit of work. While the first few teaching sessions are planned in detail, subsequent sessions are lightly sketched out, with objectives planned based on the opportunities provided by the part of the text the children will be reading or by the writing that they will be doing. It is impossible to write with complete detail at the start of the planning stage. Instead the detail needs to be added as the lessons unfold, based on a teacher's ongoing assessments, with lessons planned to meet children's changing needs. For example, in a traditional weekly planning model a teacher might have decided to teach a discrete lesson on a particular aspect of grammar. From reading children's writing, it is clear that in fact many of the class would benefit from looking at something else instead. A *sketch planned* unit has a space earmarked for a session of English language teaching, but by waiting to decide the specific focus for each session in response to assessment, the sessions can be relevant to children's needs and the level of challenge can be pitched correctly. The best teaching of English is flexible and informed by assessment; *sketch planning* allows for this without wasted planning time.

Structure of lessons

The Literacy Hour, the centrepiece of the National Literacy Strategy (1999) created as a standardised model for daily literacy teaching, didn't last very long. In many classrooms, experienced teachers saw it as being restrictive and unmanageable, actually getting in the way of good teaching and learning. However, the three-part lesson of teacher talk, independent activity and plenary is still dominant in many classrooms; a template that teachers can sometimes feel reluctant to break away from. Sometimes in three-parts is exactly the right way to structure a lesson. The opportunity to introduce a concept, allow children to show they can do it and then check their understanding through a plenary can be a brilliantly effective model. But it isn't the only model and, in good English teaching, often it isn't the best model. The arrival of the 2014 National Curriculum has led to the National Strategies, which did so much to embed the three-part lesson in schools, being 'archived'. In England Ofsted is often cited as the reason to stick to a familiar lesson structure. However, since 2012 Ofsted has made clear that inspectors are not looking for a particular style of teaching, as the previous HMCI Sir Michael Wilshaw tried to clarify:

> I also want to lay to rest the myth that inspectors want to see a certain kind of lesson. Yes, lessons should be planned, but not in an

overly complicated and formulaic way. A crowded lesson plan is as bad as a crowded curriculum. We want to see pupils engaged and learning. So if an inspector walks into a classroom and the pupils are working on an extended task for the whole time, that's fine. If a teacher is reading a play with the class and they are all engaged, that's fine too. There should be no prescription about lesson structure.

(Wilshaw, 2012)

An effective unit of work will use a range of different lesson structures because each lesson will have a different purpose and different intended outcomes.

Think and reflect

Five questions to ask when planning the structure of a lesson:

1. What do I want the children to learn/apply/practice in the session?
2. What will be the outcome of the session? Does there need to be an outcome at the end or could today's learning feed into future work?
3. How will I feedback to children about their work? How will they feedback to me about what they've learnt?
4. How can I ensure that all children are challenged and all children have the chance to achieve in the session?
5. Are there any additional opportunities for learning or developing additional skills? Oracy? Working as a team? ICT?

Appendix II is a plan for a unit of work based on the myth *The Labours of Hercules* for Year 4 (8 and 9-year-olds). Working though this plan and thinking carefully about the reasons why each element has been included is a useful way of thinking about what makes an effective text-based unit.

The Labours of Hercules – a Year 4 text-based unit

Texts studied

The unit of work is based on two wonderful versions of the story: *The Twelve Labours of Hercules* by James Riordan and Christina Balit and a retelling in *Greek Heroes* by Geraldine McCaughrean. Additional versions of *The Labours of Hercules* and non-fiction texts that provide background and context to the story are used to support the core text. These work as parallel texts, offering different perspectives on and employing different ways of sharing the same story. Many of the sections could also be told orally or shared through drama by a teacher who is confident in this way of working.

Unit objectives

The unit of work is based on the 2014 National Curriculum and the text provides a vehicle for meeting its demands: higher expectations for language comprehension in Key Stage 2, a sharper, more focused structure for teaching writing and raised expectations for teaching aspects of English language, such as grammar and punctuation.

While some learning objectives taken from the curriculum lend themselves to being taught discretely, some are too wide-ranging to be taught in just one lesson. Aims such as 'developing positive attitudes to reading and understanding what they have read' or 'increasing their familiarity with a wide range of key texts, including myths and legends' cannot be achieved in one lesson. Instead, they need to be taught continuously over time. Building a longer unit of work around a quality text can help children to meet these curriculum demands.

Before you start

A key element of comprehension is being able to match what we're reading to our knowledge of the outside world: to use our general knowledge to build a mental image of the information in the text. If we don't know anything about a particular topic, it can be very difficult to make sense of what we're reading.

For a child, studying *The Labours of Hercules* might be a richer experience if they know something about the character of Hercules. Many children will be familiar with the Disney film Hercules, which borrows from a number of myths and legends, but tells a very different story to the one in this unit. A few moments sharing some pictures of Hercules and the story of him strangling the serpents sent to kill him as a baby helps children to build a mental model as they read or listen to the story.

Outcomes

The narrative structure of *The Labours of Hercules*, a longer narrative composed of a series of shorter stories each covering a labour Hercules must complete to earn the forgiveness of the Gods, is perfect for organising an English unit on narrative writing. Children will create a book telling the story of their own labours, writing three short stories, each forming a chapter of their own book. This gives them the chance to write several short stories, each with a similar structure, in close proximity so they can act on feedback from previous stories and it allows the teacher to focus on different storytelling techniques and aspects of writing in each story.

The children will also write a character study of Hercules, providing a chance to practise having a different purpose for their writing and to demonstrate their understanding of the text. Tasks like this are also useful practice in responding to a text in writing, which is important in later schooling. In addition to written tasks, the children will also have the chance to take part in drama activities and oral retelling of the story over the course of the unit.

Sequence of lessons

As discussed above, the teaching sequence for a unit will depend on the text, the children, the teacher and the intended outcomes. As well as sharing a wonderful story with children, this unit is focused on developing narrative writing.

Lessons 1–4 – These four lessons are principally about becoming familiar with the story and beginning to understand Hercules as a character. The children have the opportunity to listen to the text read aloud and to read it themselves through shared reading. They can also learn and retell some of the stories. In this unit the focus is at a high level: that of the story itself. In other units of work the focus might be on the text itself, analysing the writing for language features or effect.

For Sessions 1 and 2, where the bulk of the shared reading takes place, the questions have been chosen for the effect they will have on the children's thinking and their ability to stimulate high-quality discussion. Other incidental questions will need to be used to clarify children's comments and move the discussion along. It is likely that there will be incidental learning about other areas, language features for example, that will occur during the sessions. When planning, it is important that teachers have the confidence to deviate from their planning to take advantage of this, while also being disciplined enough to return to the key focus of the session.

Lessons 5 and 6 – In a traditional model, where the unit is building to a piece of narrative writing, the focus in these lessons might be on capturing ideas for children's own stories. This process and then the story planning that follows it means that it could be several more days before the children are ready to write. In this adapted model (see Chapter 8), an additional piece of writing is added. The children write a character study of Hercules. This has several purposes: to ensure that children have the opportunity to write regularly, to give children another type of writing and to help the teacher assess their understanding of the text they've studied. As with all pieces of writing, children are given the opportunity to edit and improve their work in the light of feedback.

Lesson 7 – This session gives children the opportunity to plan their story. Planning should be a flexible process: as much about thinking and imagining possibilities as it is about recording ideas. While a formal story planning method, such as a story map, can be useful, model planning encompasses the broader thinking and discussing that children might do. Planning should also be presented as a starting point, ready to be deviated from as children begin writing and new ideas come to them. However, time spent planning before writing helps children to think about audience and purpose and to be in the best position to begin writing, helping them to avoid the fear of a blank page when they sit down to write.

Lessons 8–14 – In these lessons, the children work through the phases of writing three times in quick succession. Each of their short stories is preceded by a day of input from the teacher. The first focuses on descriptive writing, with the children developing their descriptive writing through the use of an image and shared writing together. In the next session, the children write their own story with an emphasis on describing the setting for their adventure, drawing on the techniques they practised the previous day. The next day, they have the opportunity to edit and redraft their work in the light of oral feedback from the teacher and their peers. This process is repeated twice more, with emphasis on learning to use dialogue to drive action and writing sentences where the reader must infer emotions from the characters' actions and words. At the end of this period the class will have had the chance to write three short stories, each with a different focus and each building on the feedback from their previous writing.

Lessons 15 onwards – The unit finishes with time for children to publish their stories. Leaving time for publishing can seem like a luxury in a busy curriculum, but creating a meaningful end product – whether a piece of writing, a performance or a presentation – is invaluable for children's motivation. If children know what they have been working towards is valued, then they're likely to invest more in it. And that will be seen in the quality of what they produce.

The unit ends with the chance for children to listen to the climax of *Labours of Hercules*. There is nothing to discuss, nothing to write, and no learning objectives. Children will simply enjoy the end to one of the most remarkable stories ever written. This too can seem like a luxury. But if, after almost a month of reading, writing and talking about *The Labours of Hercules*, we can't find time for some magic, then what is the point in building a curriculum around great books?

Why not try?

With a curriculum model that is based around text types, each unit typically builds to producing a piece of writing in that genre: a narrative, a letter or a non-chronological report. While this sustained time building to one piece of writing is vital, sometimes it makes sense for children to write several pieces of the same type of writing in quick succession. If they receive feedback in between, they can act on this, improving each version. Several individual pieces can be more motivating than redrafting the same piece several times. Some practical ideas, drawn from texts, might be:

Groups of narratives – two or more short stories that function as chapters of a longer book, as with *The Labours of Hercules* unit in Appendix II. This could also work with stories such as *The Odyssey*, set on a series of islands (using *The Adventures of Odysseus* by Hugh Lupton and Daniel Morden) or contemporary books made up of individual stories featuring the same character such as *Mango and Bambang*.

Poetry anthologies – children can write several different types of poems (for example, haiku, calligrams, acrostics, rhyming couplets, etc.) around a theme – nature, the sea or the local area – and then publish these as an individual anthology. This gives children the opportunity to consider how the form of a poem and the language work together to share meaning.

Letters and replies – rather than writing one letter, children can write an initial letter and then the reply. This helps to practise letter conventions, but also gives them the opportunity to write in different fictional voices. Good example texts might be *The Jolly Postman*, *Dear Greenpeace* or *The Last Polar Bears*.

This chapter has outline some approaches to organising a text-based unit of work for English lessons. It is important to emphasise that the best lessons are not devised and written by someone else: great teaching and learning don't come in pre-written programmes, created and resourced ready to be 'delivered' – that's just not how it works. Chapters 3 and 4 have considered the curriculum vehicles that can be used for creating rich and meaningful sequences of learning from great books. But books come alive in the hands of teachers. No matter how well-planned a curriculum is, it is the teaching that will decide whether it is successful or not. With this idea in mind, Parts 2 and 3 of *Teaching English by the Book* focus on the teaching of reading and writing.

In summary

- An overview of the texts that children will study as they move through the school ensures progression and entitlement and avoids repetition

- Allocating the texts that teachers *must* share with children can be restrictive for confident teachers of English and can prevent them from teaching the texts they might teach best

- Coverage is the enemy of good learning – a well-planned curriculum leaves room for flexibility and time to revisit elements that children haven't understood the first time around

- A three-part model of familiarisation with a type of text, planning and then creating is useful, but teaching might benefit from following this pattern across a longer unit. Instead, the three stages might be revisited repeatedly over the course of the text-based unit

- Lessons should be structured for a purpose and not every lesson will fit the same pattern

Bibliography

DfE (2013) *National Curriculum in England: Primary Curriculum*. London: DfE.

DfES (1999) *National Literacy Strategy*. London: DfES.

Wilshaw, M. (2012) We can do better, in *Times Educational Supplement*, 30 March 2012 – www.tes.com/news/tes-archive/tes-publication/we-can-do-better (accessed 14 February 2017).

Literature

Charlotte's Web by E. B. White
Dear Greenpeace by Simon James
Dogger by Shirley Hughes
Greek Heroes by Geraldine McCaughrean
Mango and Bambang by Polly Faber and Clara Vulliamy
Night of the Gargoyles by Eve Bunting
Not Now Bernard by David McKee
Oi Frog! by Kes Grey and Jim Field
Railhead by Philip Reeve
Rooftoppers by Katherine Rundell
The Adventures of Odysseus by Hugh Lupton and Daniel Morden
The Enemy by Davide Cali and Serge Bloch
The Iron Man by Ted Hughes
The Island by Armin Greder
The Jolly Postman by Janet and Allan Ahlberg
The Last Polar Bears by Harry Horse
The Twelve Labours of Hercules by James Ford

PART 2

Teaching reading by the book

A model for teaching reading

Reading is a complicated business and learning to make sense of the words on a page or screen involves a combination of complex skills. The dominant model used to describe the process of reading in recent years has been the Simple View of Reading, first proposed by Gough and Tunmer (1986). This model for the reading process was popularised by Rose's *Review of the Teaching of Early Reading* (2006), which has been very influential in guiding national policy on reading in England, not least providing the model used by the 2014 National Curriculum.

Despite its name, the Simple View of Reading doesn't suggest that reading is a simple process; rather it attempts to provide a simple way of making sense of a very complicated process. According to the Simple View of Reading there are two key components to reading: language comprehension and visual word recognition. Both of these elements are necessary to be a skilled reader.

Language comprehension is the process of understanding language; this might be the words we read or spoken language. Visual word recognition is concerned with decoding: the process of recognising the words on a page or screen. The reader doesn't understand the text, but to read words well they just need to recognise the individual sounds or words. Reading is the product of these two elements working together and neither on its own is sufficient for skilled reading.

Language comprehension

Language comprehension refers to the understanding of spoken or written language. The development of this element precedes word-reading, with children's language comprehension beginning with a growing understanding of spoken language and the texts that are read aloud to them. It continues to develop while children are learning to decode the words on the page, again by listening to spoken language and to texts being read aloud. Once children can decode with confidence, development in their comprehension comes from the texts that they read too.

Mental models

When we listen to or read a text, we rarely remember the exact words and phrases as they have been written. Instead, we construct a *mental model* of what we've read – an image in our head of what the text is telling us and what is happening. The clearer and more detailed this mental model is, the better our understanding of the text is likely to be. Our mental model develops as we encounter new ideas and new information in the text. It is constructed from information explicitly stated in the text and inferences we make from drawing on our existing knowledge to fill in the gaps in our understanding. For example:

> *He stepped out of his front door and stopped abruptly. His satchel fell to the ground and his face drained of all colour.*

Here, we begin to build a mental model of a male character leaving his home. We might infer the character has seen something that has shocked him and immediately we begin to speculate what that might be. Because he has a satchel, we might guess that it is a boy. We may already have had a clue from our previous knowledge of the story – what has happened so far, or from reading the blurb or looking at the front cover, perhaps. As the text continues and we read on, we will find out more about the scene and this will feed into and further develop our mental model, helping the reader to build a more accurate picture.

Building a robust mental model sits at the heart of good comprehension and there are a number of factors that are useful to consider when supporting children to make meaning from a text:

- Background knowledge
- Vocabulary development
- Inference
- Comprehension monitoring
- Text structure

Background knowledge

Building a robust mental model depends on our existing knowledge as well as the new information shared by the text. Every reader brings their existing knowledge to the texts that they read, incorporating the new information from the text into their existing schema. The greater our knowledge about a particular subject, the easier it is to form a mental model. Research suggests that strong background knowledge is closely correlated with reading comprehension, both if the reader has specific knowledge about the subject that they are reading about (Recht and Leslie, 1988) and if they have wider general knowledge (Cunningham and Stanovich, 1997). Take these sentences about cosmological science:

> *Inflationary expansion ceases when an inflation field relinquishes its stored energy and negative pressure. Because of the effects of quantum mechanics, the amount of spatial expansion at different locations will vary, leading to inhomogeneities in space.*

While a general reader may know the meaning of (most of) the individual words, it is difficult for someone with no background knowledge of this area to make sense of the text. There is no existing body of knowledge in which to embed it. This is true of the reading that children do: a child who is very knowledgeable about dinosaurs will be able to make sense of a book that a peer who isn't knowledgeable about dinosaurs would find very challenging, even if their current reading ability is similar or not yet as strong (Yekovich *et al.*, 1990).

Background knowledge isn't just important for understanding the broader implications of a text – picturing the setting or putting a new idea into a wider context – it can also help readers to make sense of the individual words:

> *At the Battle of Agincourt, Henry V led the English army that fought* **with** *France.*
> *With the dark clouds of war enveloping Europe, Britain had no choice but to fight* **with** *France.*

The word *with* means the opposite in these two examples of non-fiction writing: against or alongside. Even if a reader understands enough to build a mental model without some background knowledge, it is possible to misunderstand and build an incorrect mental model.

Vocabulary development

Not surprisingly, knowledge of vocabulary correlates highly with successful reading comprehension: if we know what the individual words mean, we're far more likely to be able to make meaning from the text as a whole (Carroll, 1993). Our *receptive vocabulary* is the set of words of which we know the meaning, even if we don't make use of them in our everyday speech. There are two aspects to receptive vocabulary: breadth and depth. The breadth of our vocabulary – how many words we know – is important, but perhaps not as important as the depth of vocabulary – how well we know each word and its meaning (Tannenbaum *et al.*, 2006). Our knowledge of each word isn't binary, instead ranging from having heard a word before but being unsure of its meaning, to being completely familiar with a word. Effective vocabulary teaching needs to support children to develop the depth of their word knowledge, as well as simply introducing them to plenty of words.

The relationship between vocabulary and comprehension is reciprocal, with the two aspects supporting one another. Children with a well-developed vocabulary are able to read more-complex texts, which introduces them to new words, further enriching their vocabulary. This is often referred to as 'the Matthew Effect': a term borrowed from sociology that is often succinctly paraphrased as 'the rich get richer' (Stanovich, 1986).

A broad and deep receptive vocabulary enables readers to take new ideas and fit them into their existing knowledge. This is true if the words come from a text that children read for themselves or if they are listening to text being read aloud. One reason for the strong relationship between vocabulary and comprehension is that a rich knowledge of word meanings supports children to make inferences.

Inference

Some the information in a text that is needed to build a mental model is likely to be given explicitly:

> *It was winter.*
> or
> *Sam was angry.*

Here, the reader doesn't need to read between the lines in order to understand the meaning. The work has been done already for the reader. In all but the simplest texts, however, at least some information is left for the reader to infer, making sense of details that are implied or making links to their knowledge beyond the book:

> *At this time of year, the frost lay thick as a carpet.*
> or
> *Sam clenched and unclenched her fists, counting to ten in her head just as her dad had taught her.*

This is especially true of the rich literary texts that can sit so successfully at the heart of the primary curriculum. Being adept at making inferences is key for effective comprehension.

Teaching of inference can often focus on drawing children's attention to the aspects of inference that have been deliberately included by an author. This might be to build suspense in a story or the use of figurative language to make a description rich and interesting – the 'showing not telling' that teachers often try to share with children as an example of mature writing. This is called *elaborative inference* or *authorial inference*. These types of inferences are important for building an understanding of a text and can help children to see how a writer makes language choices to create a specific effect. However, the types of inferences that readers need to make in order to understand a text can also happen on a far simpler level.

Local cohesion and *coherence inferences* are where constructing meaning relies on making a link between ideas in different parts of the text. These are often, but not always, made automatically. Examples include recognising what a particular pronoun refers to:

> *The squirrel sniffed at the nut and then carried it away.*

Here, understanding relies on knowing that the 'it' is the nut. This is relatively simple, but can still cause problems for beginner readers, especially those expending a great deal of processing power on decoding the letters on the page.

Another example might be a reader understanding the meaning of different sentence structures. For example, being able to follow what has happened in a sentence with an embedded clause:

> *The blue trousers which fitted better than my red ones were the pair I chose in the end.*

Here, the reader need to identify that the embedded clause (*which fitted better than my red ones*) is simply giving additional information and it is the blue trousers that were chosen. This can be challenging for developing readers, especially if, as in this case, the embedded clause is not demarcated by commas. Effective comprehension depends as much on understanding how grammar works as it does on knowledge of vocabulary. In the primary classroom, grammar and punctuation are often viewed through the prism of writing, but they are also significant factors in children's reading development too.

As well as inferences for local cohesion, such as understanding different sentence structures, readers will often need to make wider, global coherence inferences that connect different parts of the text, for example linking a character's actions to wider events in a text:

> *By the time he reached the front of the queue, the shelves were empty. Patrick began to cry.*

Here, a reader would need to infer that the setting is probably a shop and whatever Patrick was queuing for was important or coveted highly, as he is upset that he couldn't buy it. This information might be given before the reader reaches these lines, or be held back until after, but the reader needs to understand and feed ideas from different parts of the text together to build a successful mental model.

Think and reflect

Considering your own school or classroom:

- How often do children have the opportunity to think about, discuss and practise the local cohesion and coherence inferences that they need to make in order to understand a text?

Comprehension monitoring

As they read or listen to a text, children with well-developed comprehension skills integrate new information into the mental model they are constructing. If the next idea they encounter makes sense, it helps to add to or refine the image they are building. If it doesn't, then they need to stop and check they've read correctly and diagnose what has gone wrong. Helping children to develop an awareness of when they've understood something and when they haven't as they read is vital in helping them to become independent readers. While reading and self-monitoring understanding is vital for language comprehension, it may also be important for wider learning. Developing an awareness of whether new ideas fit with our existing knowledge base could help to develop critical thinking and support learning across the rest of the curriculum (Oakhill *et al.*, 2005).

Text structure

Different types of texts each have different conventions and structures. Children who have a good knowledge of these structures, both narratives and the various non-fiction forms, use this knowledge to support their comprehension monitoring. With narratives, a good knowledge of how stories work, built up through listening and reading, can help children to identify when they've missed something or misunderstood: when a story doesn't meet their expectations (for example, there appears to be a diversion from the 'beginning, middle and end' structure they are familiar with) they know to stop and check that it is the story not behaving as they expect and not their understanding that is at fault. Knowledge of structure can also help children to know where to look for information in a text – key details at the start of a newspaper report, for example, or a description of the setting at the start of a story.

Visual word recognition

Visual word recognition is the ability to recognise and, if required, pronounce the words on a page or screen. Stuart and Stainthorp state:

> Visual word recognition depends on three kinds of linked representations: orthographic, semantic and phonological. An orthographic representation is the stored spelling pattern of a word. A semantic representation is the stored meaning(s) of a word. A phonological representation is the stored sound pattern of a word.
>
> (Stuart and Stainthorp, 2016)

As seen in Chapter 2, the phonological element is often taught discretely in English schools through explicit phonics sessions, followed up in small group reading or the texts children are given to take home and read independently. This matches the recommendations of the Rose Review:

> It is therefore crucial to teach phonic work systematically, regularly and explicitly, because children are highly unlikely to work out this relationship for themselves. It cannot be left to chance, or for children to ferret out, on their own, how the alphabetic code works.
>
> (Rose, 2006)

The types of book that support discrete development in word-reading are likely to be decodable texts that have been written for children to use their developing word-reading skills in context. Stuart and Stainthorp note:

> Children gain a sense of mastery from being able to read texts independently, a sense of 'I can do this!' which is so important in motivating them to read. However, the down sides of a carefully controlled vocabulary include limitations to the richness of the story, which might have negative effects on motivation.
>
> (Stuart and Stainthorp, 2016)

Decodable texts are very different to the rich literature that is advocated in this book: books to be shared, to drive discussion and comprehension and to build text-based units of work around. But decodable texts will help children to develop their word-reading skills in a systematic way and could help them to feel the sense of success that comes with reading a book independently.

Fluent word-reading is vital: it is very difficult to develop a love of reading if you are struggling with the mechanics of the process. A child might love books and they might enjoy being read to, but to become an independent reader and have the freedom to follow their own interests, developing strong word-reading is important. It is also important that systematic phonics teaching sits within a rich text-based environment. While children are learning to word-read, they should continue to have a wide range of books and stories read to them, forming the basis for English lessons and reading for enjoyment. They should also have access to a wide range of texts to look through and enjoy independently, even if they cannot yet read the words.

In a school where children's reading development is well-planned and driven by a clear rationale to help every child to become a confident and competent reader, systematic teaching of decoding, comprehension teaching using texts that are read aloud and reading for enjoyment through rich reading experiences shouldn't work in competition with one other. Instead, all three are leading towards the same aim: helping a child become a lifelong reader.

Think and reflect

- When considering how children develop their word-reading in your school or classroom, do they:
- Have the opportunity to learn to word-read in a systematic way that makes the alphabetic code clear?
- Have the opportunity to use their word-reading skills across a range of contexts?
- Have access to a wide range of rich and engaging texts to look at themselves, be read aloud to them and discuss?

A 'slightly-more-complicated view of reading'

The Simple View of Reading provides a useful model to explore the process of learning to read. However, being a reader in the widest sense is more than visual word-reading and language comprehension. There are a whole raft of skills and behaviours that make a child reader, rather than simply someone who *can* read. These include:

Fluency and reading stamina

If children are to become confident readers, they need to be able to read fluently and to be able to concentrate for extended periods of time, demonstrating good reading stamina.

Fluency is the ability to read a text accurately and quickly and, if reading aloud, with appropriate expression and intonation. Research suggests that development of fluency may be linked to both reading comprehension (Cutting and Scarborough, 2006) and word-reading (Holliman *et al.*, 2016). The accuracy and speed aspects of fluency are important for comprehension, as fluent readers do not have to labour over decoding the individual words – something which ties up valuable working memory. Fluency allows them to focus on making meaning from the text. The prosodic elements of fluency, such as intonation, expression, tempo and pausing appropriately, can be a useful way of demonstrating comprehension – a teacher can gauge a child's under-standing by the emphasis they give to words and phrases and their pronunciation of different words (for example, reading 'console' as either a device for playing games or as comforting someone).

While fluency could be placed under the word recognition element of the Simple View of Reading, this isn't always the case in practice, especially as children move further up the school. The attention that is given to children's reading fluency as they begin to learn to read isn't always maintained and the focus of reading teaching can move to com-prehension and analysis of texts. As the texts that children read become more challenging, it is important that teachers ensure children can read these texts fluently.

Reading stamina (the ability to read and concentrate on a text of the appropriate challenge for a sustained period of time) is also cru-cial for successful reading. Reading stamina can be seen as an out-come of confident reading: it is very difficult to read for a prolonged period if you are struggling with the process of reading. It is also linked to the text itself, as it is far easier to be motivated if you are 'lost in a good book'. However, reading stamina builds with time and practice and, like any activity that requires concentration, can be developed.

The desire to read

Learning to read is vital. If children are to succeed at secondary school and go on to choose what they wish to do in later life, they need to leave primary school as confident readers, reflected in both aspects of the Simple View of Reading. But, if a child *can* read but then don't *choose* to read, they are missing out on all the benefits that being a reader brings. These include academic benefits – better general knowledge, improved reading outcomes and even an impact on vocabulary, spelling and mathematics – but also that reading can be a pleasurable thing to do.

There is a clear two-way relationship between these aspects of reading: it is very difficult to develop a love of reading if you struggle with word-reading or comprehension, but if the teaching of reading only focuses on the technical aspects, without thought to sharing the pleasures of reading, then a key aspect of what it means to become a reader is missing.

In the next two chapters, we will consider some practical ways for developing these two aspects of reading using a text-based approach. Chapter 5 will focus on teaching children to become confident readers and Chapter 6 will consider how we can encourage children to read.

In summary

- The Simple View of Reading outlines two interrelated aspects of reading: visual word recognition and language comprehension
- Language comprehension can be affected by a number of factors, including background knowledge, breadth and depth of vocabulary and the ability to make inferences

(continued)

In summary (*continued*)

- The two aspects of the Simple View of Reading are important for a child to be able to read, but they are not sufficient for a child to become a reader. This slightly-more complicated view of reading depends on word-reading, comprehension and also other attributes such as fluency, reading stamina and the desire to read

Bibliography

Carroll, J. B. (1993) *Human Cognitive Abilities: A Survey of Factor-Analytic Studies.* New York: Cambridge University Press.

Cunningham, A. E. and Stanovich, K. (1997) Early reading acquisition and its relation to reading experience and ability 10 years later. *Developmental Psychology*, 33 (6), 934–945.

Cutting, L. E. and Scarborough, H. S. (2006) Prediction of reading comprehension: Relative contributions of word recognition, language proficiency, and other cognitive skills can depend on how comprehension is measured. *Scientific Studies of Reading*, 10 (3), 277–299.

Gough, P. B. and Tunmer, W. E. (1986) Decoding, reading, and reading disability. *RASE: Remedial and Special Education*, 7 (1), 6–10.

Holliman, A. J., Gutiérrez Palma, N., Critten, S., Wood, C., Cunnane, H. and Pillinger, C. (2016) Examining the independent contribution of prosodic sensitivity to word reading and spelling in early readers. *Reading and Writing*, 30 (3), 509–521.

Oakhill, J., Hartt, J. and Samols, D. (2005) Levels of comprehension monitoring and working memory in good and poor comprehenders, *Reading and Writing*, 18 (7–9), 657–713.

Recht, D. R. and Leslie, L. (1988) Effect of prior knowledge on good and poor readers' memory of text. *Journal of Educational Psychology*, 80 (1988), 16–20.

Rose, J. (2006) *Independent Review of the Teaching of Early Reading.* Nottingham: DfES.

Stanovich, K. E. (1986) Matthew effects in reading: some consequences of individual differences in the acquisition of literacy. *Reading Research Quarterly*, 21 (4), 360–407.

Stuart, M. and Stainthorp, R. (2016) *Reading Development and Teaching.* London: Sage.

Tannenbaum, K. R., Torgesen, J. K., and Wagner, R. K. (2006) Relationships between word knowledge and reading comprehension in third grade children. *Scientific Studies of Reading*, 10 (4), 381–398.

Yekovich, F. R., Walker, C. H., Ogle, L. T. and Thompson, M. A. (1990) The influence of domain knowledge on inferencing in low-aptitude individuals. In A. C. Graesser and H. Bower (eds) *The Psychology of Learning and Motivation: Inferences and Text Comprehension*, 24, 175–196. New York: Academic Press.

Teaching reading

Becoming a reader

Of course it's possible to learn to read without using books, but it would be a very odd way to go about it. Therefore, this chapter is concerned not so much with *why* we should use great books to help children to become confident, competent readers, but exactly *how* we might do that most effectively. The three factors to consider are:

- The curriculum for reading
- The strategies and approaches for teaching reading
- The choice of texts that children read

These three factors depend heavily on one another and benefit from being considered concurrently. Chapter 1 addressed choosing the right book and Chapters 2 and 3 considered how these might be organised into a coherent curriculum. This Chapter will look at some practical ways to support the development of children's reading using rich texts.

In the last chapter, we considered the role language comprehension, word recognition and attitude to reading play in children becoming confident and keen readers. Teaching reading in schools needs to focus on developing one or more of these elements. This chapter will address:

- Modelling the reading process
- Asking questions
- Developing vocabulary
- Supporting background knowledge

Modelling the reading process

Shared writing is a popular strategy in many primary classrooms: the teacher models the process of writing, showing children how a skilled writer creates a text. The modelling of reading in this way is far less common, but is every bit as important. Teachers can share the process of reading, making explicit how a mature reader makes sense from a text, navigates an unfamiliar word or infers an idea from the text. This is the key to helping children see how reading works and how accomplished readers behave when they read. This can be done through the teacher thinking aloud – providing a running commentary as they read. They might also stop to ask questions or to discuss a point, but the key aim is to share how they make sense of what they read, as in this example using in the opening passage of *The Call of the Wild* by Jack London:

> *Buck did not read the newspapers, or he would have known that trouble was brewing, not alone for himself, but for every tide-water dog, strong of muscle and with warm, long hair, from Puget Sound to San Diego. Because men, groping in the Arctic darkness, had found a yellow metal, and because steamship and transportation companies were booming the find, thousands of men were rushing into the Northland. These men wanted dogs, and the dogs they wanted were heavy dogs, with strong muscles by which to toil, and furry coats to protect them from the frost.*

As the teacher and children are reading it together, the teacher could comment on:

- How ideas in the text and ideas from children's background knowledge are combined to make meaning:

  > *I'm not sure when the book is set, but they had steamships, so I think that might be a while ago. It's not ancient history, but it isn't the present either.*

- The meaning of any unfamiliar of words:

> *I'm not exactly sure what 'toil' means, but I suppose it could mean lifting something heavy or some other kind of hard work as the texts says that you need strong muscles to do it.*

- The reason particular words or phrases may have been chosen by the author:

> *I like the phrase 'groping in the Arctic darkness'. It really captures that the men are looking for something that is hard to find and it also tells you where they're going to be looking.*

- Inferences required to help the text make sense: both local cohesive inference such as clarifying to whom a pronoun refers or more general inferences needed to make meaning:

> *Well, the text doesn't say who Buck is, but I wonder if he is a dog? That would make sense as he couldn't read a newspaper and trouble would be brewing for him as he might be about to be sent away to toil in the Northland. I'll read on and see.*

Asking questions aloud and then answering them can be particularly effective:

> *I wonder which country it is set in? It mentions the Arctic, but I think that is where they're sending the dogs. It also says San Diego. I wonder where that is? Ah, I know: it's in the USA because I've heard of a basketball team from there.*

As can making a deliberate mistake in your understanding, resulting in howls of protest from the children:

> *Yellow metal? So they've found gold. And they need strong dogs to help find it. I expect they'll get the dogs to dig it out of the ground with their paws.*

The area of the reading curriculum where the modelling happens can vary. It might be through shared reading, with the whole class reading a text together, small-group reading or an adult reading with an individual child who would particularly benefit from this. What is important is that, although it happens regularly, it shouldn't happen every time an adult reads aloud. Occasionally we want to show children how being a reader works, but most of the time, especially when we're reading aloud, we want them to be swept away by the story. No one needs a running commentary modelling the reading process in the penultimate chapter of *Charlotte's Web*.

Asking questions

Effective questioning sits at the heart of good teaching. This is especially true of reading comprehension. The traditional model of a child reading a text and then answering a series of questions on it is a long way from the rich, discursive questioning that drives the effective teaching of reading. Chapter 10 explores in detail how discussion and dialogue can support children's learning, but in specific relation to teaching reading, a teacher needs to consider:

Range of question types

The benefits of planning a range of different question types and then using these to drive discussion around a book are familiar to many teachers. This includes questions to check literal understanding, inference, empathy and opinion. These are often divided into closed and open questions – broadly defined as questions with one answer and questions with more than one answer. While research (Harrison and Howard, 2009) suggests that a move towards more open questions is beneficial, it has also been suggested that the authenticity of the questions should be considered – whether questions allow for more than one answer, including answers that have not been anticipated by the teacher (Tennant *et al.*, 2016). These are questions that require a genuine answer, rather than one the teacher is expecting which can be definitely right or wrong. That's not to say that questions with a definite answer are not useful for checking understanding, but questions that feed in to genuine dialogue and ones that are asked out of interest can be key to building comprehension.

Cascading questions

An effective approach to planning questions is to think about a cascade of questions that begins with a broad question or statement leading to discussion, with additional questions (both open and closed) driving the discussion and prompting further thinking. These questions can be roughly planned; they are designed to draw out a particular teaching point, but require some flexibility on the part of the teacher, too, so that teachers are responsive to children's ideas. For example, a cascade of questions about *Treasure Island* by Robert Louis Stevenson might look like:

Opening question

In Chapter 1, what does the author tell us about Billy Bones?

Follow-up questions

What might his 'hands ragged and scarred' tell us about him?

What does Stevenson mean when he says: 'seemed like a mate or skipper, accustomed to be obeyed or to strike'.

What does the chapter tell us about Billy Bones' past?

Where might Billy Bones have come from?

How does Jim feel about Billy Bones? How do you know?

What might happen next?

All of the follow-up questions help children to arrive at a full answer to the opening question. Some of these questions can be planned (after the teacher has read the chapter), while others will occur spontaneously.

Generic sets of questions

There are many sources of generic questions to ask about a text which are available as published schemes, sets of cards or as downloadable resources found online. It is suggested that these questions could be applied to any text. Teachers should be extremely cautious about the use of these: banks of sample questions or question stems can be useful as a starting point, but they then need to be tailored to a particular text if they are to be authentic and useful for driving reflection and learning.

Think and reflect

Compare these generic questions designed for any text to a set of specific questions and think about which is most likely to support children's understanding.

In small group reading, the children read the poems *For the Fallen* by Laurence Binyon and *Dulce et Decorum Est* by Wilfred Owen (both of which can be found by searching online).

Generic questions

1. Who wrote the text you read?
2. What happens in the text?
3. What did the author's purpose seem to be?
4. What is the theme of the text?
5. What is the author's point of view on any relevant theme or issue?
6. Did you like the text? Why/why not?

Text-specific questions

1. Do the two poems take the same view of fighting in a war?

(continued)

Think and reflect (*continued*)

2. What does *For the Fallen* suggest will happen to the soldiers who gave their life?

   – What will they do 'when we are dust'?
   – Would Wilfred Owen have agreed with this?

3. What does '*dulce et decorum est pro patria mori*' mean?

   – Why does the poet describe this phrase as 'the ultimate lie'?
   – Would the author of *For the Fallen* have agreed that it was 'the ultimate lie'?

4. How might the wartime experiences of the two poets have shaped their poetry and their ideas?

5. Do you agree with either poet? Or do you hold a different view?

Children asking questions

The questions the children ask, both in discussion and to themselves as they read, can be as important as the questions the teacher asks. Children often need support in devising questions. This can be offered through modelling the sort of questions that they could ask (as above) or through displaying question stems or example questions in the classroom or discussing them beforehand; however, these are likely to be generic questions, rather than text-specific ones.

One of the simplest and most effective questions children can ask themselves is: am I able to summarise what has happened? This does not need to be a written task, and in fact it is more effective if it isn't; it can be as simple as one child turning to a partner. Summarising helps children to articulate the mental model they have made of a text and to check that it is accurate. Challenging children to make connections (simply asking them, 'how does this sentence connect with what we've read so far?') can support them to reflect on any new information the sentence provides.

Questions before, during and after

In addition to questions that follow a text, asking questions before and during the children's reading can be helpful for comprehension. Questions asked before help to build prediction skills and can activate prior knowledge. Questions during reading help children to reflect on their understanding: building comprehension monitoring and stopping them from racing through the text without understanding.

Statements not questions

Although this section is about questions, statements can also be a useful starting point for discussion, breaking up the pattern of question–answer–response that can dominate classroom discourse. Presenting a statement as a starting point, rather than a question, can lead to greater engagement, especially if it is a stimulating statement that divides opinion. After reading *A Well-Mannered Young Wolf* by Jean Leroy and Mattieu Maudet we might state:

> *The wolf is right to eat the chicken and the rabbit.*

Or after Charles Dickens' *Great Expectations* we might argue that:

> *Pip would have had a better life if he had never met Abel Magwitch.*

Both statements would make an engaging alternative to a series of questions. As with teacher modelling, effective use of questioning or statements should happen right across the reading curriculum.

Vocabulary development

There is a close relationship between the breadth and depth of children's vocabulary and their reading comprehension. One of the most effective ways of building children's vocabulary is the simplest and most enjoyable: reading (Cunningham, 2005). Encouraging children to read as widely as possible in their own time and by reading aloud to them, especially challenging texts or books that they might not choose to read themselves, can directly support vocabulary growth and, by implication, reading comprehension.

There are also a number of other ways that children's vocabulary development can be directly supported:

Choose the most useful words to teach directly

Learning word lists or initiatives like 'Word of the Week' can be effective (although at a rate of 39 new words each year, it might take a while), but how do we go about choosing the most useful words? One approach is by thinking about the 'tiers' words fall into.

Beck *et al.* (2002) divide the words we use in school into three tiers:

- Tier one words are commonly used in spoken language (e.g. cat, run, drawing, strong)
- Tier two words are found in more mature written texts (valuable, discuss, complication, surge)
- Tier three words are technical words: the language of the curriculum (vertebrate, simile, Neolithic)

Tier one words are commonly learnt through speech, while tier three words are often taught explicitly in lessons at school. If vocabulary teaching can focus on tier two words, children will have access to these words, supporting them as writers and readers. An internet search for 'tier two words' will provide plenty of word lists and teaching ideas (but do check it's not a list from the USA or you'll end up with a class full of children using American spellings).

Use etymology and morphology to help children to unlock the meaning of words

Explicitly teaching word-knowledge through morphology and etymology can be invaluable. If children understand the way different root words, suffixes and prefixes combine to make meaning (morphology) or if they have a knowledge of where words have come from and the 'families' of words to which they belong (etymology), they are more likely to be able to work out the meaning of a word when they come across it independently. Knowing the Latin root 'fract' means 'to break', for example, might help children to make sense of words such as 'fracture' or 'fraction'. Knowing the suffix '-ous' often denotes being in possession of a certain quality might help children to understand 'courageous' or 'spacious'.

Plan for repetition

In order for a word to become part of a child's receptive vocabulary (a word they recognise the meaning of) children need to encounter a word many times (Cain *et al.*, 2003). Re-reading the same picture books or sharing books, films and online resources on the same topic can support this, as can an integrated curriculum model, where children have the opportunity to use the same words and phrases in different areas of the curriculum and these are reflected in the books that they read – for example, studying the Ancient Romans while reading Rosemary Sutcliff's *Eagle of the Ninth* in English or learning about the theory of evolution in science while reading *What Mr Darwin Saw* by Mick Manning.

Think beyond synonyms

In the primary classroom, words are often presented as being synonyms of one another – words that share the same meaning. In fact, this is rarely the case. Different words might have very similar meanings, but might not be able to be used in the same context. The thesaurus suggests *bad*, *naughty* and *immoral* are all synonyms of one another, but while we might come across a character in a story admonishing their 'bad dog' or 'naughty dog', we rarely encounter an immoral dog. Children need to be taught to think beyond words as having interchangeable meanings and instead to reflect on their precise meaning. This is a gradual process that builds over time. It also involves children having the confidence to try new words and make mistakes, which depends on the culture of the classroom.

Why not try?

Bookmarks for collecting words

Children can be given a bookmark with a blank table on it. If they come across a new or unfamiliar word as they're reading, they jot it down in one of the cells on their bookmark. Because the bookmark sits in their book, children haven't got to hunt around for a notebook; it is an immediate process.

Having the bookmark also reminds them to keep an eye out for interesting words as they read. The real value, however, comes from putting time aside each week for children to bring out their bookmarks and share the words they've found with their classmates. They can discuss the meaning of unfamiliar words, working towards a meaning together; swap words that they like and the whole class can look at some of their findings with the teacher, discussing the word and its meaning and uses. This approach gives two benefits: firstly, it supports children to look for interesting examples of language in the books they read independently and secondly, it provides a vehicle to talk about vocabulary in a meaningful, authentic way.

Supporting background knowledge

For children to understand a text they need to be able to link it to their existing knowledge. The more we know about a topic, the easier it is to understand what you read. It is clearly impossible to prepare children for everything they need to know to understand a text and different children will arrive at a text with very different bodies of knowledge. There are a number of things teachers can do help children to support them:

Start with the book itself

Asking children to comment on the cover of a book and asking them about the title are both simple ways of prompting them to activate their background knowledge; helping to make connections across wider reading. Prior reading can be unlocked through simple questions, such as:

- Have you met these characters before?
- Have you read anything by this author before?
- Does this book remind you of anything you've read before?
- What sort of book might this be?

Encourage children to think what they might already know about a text by starting with key words that are likely to be crucial in helping them to form a mental model. Of course, some children might not have a great deal of background knowledge about a topic, so they might benefit from this being a brief activity before moving on.

Judicious pre-teaching

Pre-teaching some key background information can help children to understand what they read and provide a deeper understanding of a text. Pre-teaching might take the form of sharing:

Key facts – this is important for non-fiction: the more we know about a topic – the Solar System, for example – the more complicated information we can understand. It also has an impact on our understanding of fiction. Knowing that England has never had a King James III and that the Channel Tunnel didn't exist in 1832 tells the reader that *The Wolves of Willoughby Chase* isn't set in the real past, but in a fantasy version of England.

Another story – if we're sharing the story of Shakespeare's *Julius Caesar*, then having some knowledge about how the Romans drove out their last king and established the senate to rule over Rome and knowing that the king's bodyguard, Brutus, played an important part in this revolution helps children to understand the dilemma his ancestor faces when we meet him in the story. Similarly, revisiting the character of the Big Bad Wolf in various fairy tales before reading *Good Little Wolf* by Nadia Shireen allows the reader to think about whether his behaviour meets our expectations or not.

Non-fiction – Likewise, reading non-fiction alongside a narrative or poem can be useful to inform children's understanding. Reading about the air raids on London during World War II alongside reading *Goodnight Mr Tom* by Michelle Magorian supports the understanding of both texts.

An experience – providing a real experience before reading can be important in helping to stimulate their imagination – whether that is visiting a wood before listening to *Little Red Riding Hood* or plunging their hands into a bowl of icy water before opening up *Shackleton's Journey* by William Grill. Of course we often can't have the real experience described in a book – sailing on a pirate ship or riding a magical unicorn – and this is one of the very reasons we choose to read and why reading is so beneficial for children: it transports them to worlds they could never visit in real life.

Images or pictures – It isn't always practical to get on a coach and take children to the seaside before you read *Dover Beach*, so a film clip or some sound effects of the sea will sometimes be a more achievable primer for approaching a text. Images can help children to picture the setting of a story; a short film recreation of Victorian London before reading Eleanor Updale's *Montmorency* supports children to picture the world of the story.

Building background knowledge – While these approaches can help with understanding a specific text, much of the reading children will do now and in later life will be self-directed and pre-teaching will be impossible.

One of the most useful things we can do to support children's comprehension is help to build a rich background of knowledge. This means giving them access to a genuine knowledge-rich curriculum at school – not simply memorising a list of facts, dates or vocabulary, but giving children the chance to learn about the world they live in: its history, geography and people. This should include opportunities to apply their growing knowledge in open-ended ways and make links between the things they have learnt in different areas of the curriculum. It means building on and valuing the knowledge that children bring from home and develop through their outside interests and doing everything we can to encourage children to read as widely as possible.

Think and reflect

Making meaning from a text might depend on making an inference, it might depend on background knowledge and it might depend on knowing the meaning of a specific word. Usually, it will depend on a combination of all of these.

Comprehension isn't a list of generic skills to be taught and learnt; instead it is the endpoint – comprehension is understanding the text.

As a result, we might expect teaching to start from the text itself, rather than from a ladder of skills. Research suggests that explicit teaching of comprehension skills can be an effective way of supporting children's understanding, especially for those children who the study judged to be 'less-skilled readers' (Elleman, 2017). However, a short period of explicit instruction appears to be as effective as prolonged practice. If we want children to become confident readers, initial teaching of these skills followed by the chance to read lots of different texts, each time asking them to find meaning, might be an effective way to go about it. This is where a well-planned text-based curriculum comes into its own. Over the course of their time at school, children have the chance to read widely, to discuss the texts they read and to practise making mental models of different types of text, building their vocabulary and knowledge slowly over time.

(continued)

Think and reflect (*continued*)

There is no substitute for it. There is no shortcut. If we want children to become readers in the widest sense, it takes time and patience. But it's worth it.

Desire to read

In this chapter we have considered some practical strategies for developing children's reading, but we have failed to mention the most important strategy of all: reading. Of all of the ways we can support children's development in reading, none comes close to its effectiveness as reading itself. Once children can decode confidently, giving them time to read and access to rich and motivating texts is the most significant factor in their development as a reader. As Stephen Krashen notes:

> While it may not be true that everything that is good for you is pleasant, the most effective way of building literacy happens to be the most pleasant.
>
> (Krashen, 2004)

Chapter 6 will consider some ways that schools and teachers can support children to read widely and often.

In summary

- Modelling the reading process is a key approach to teaching reading. It allows children to see what a skilled reader does to make meaning from the text
- Rather than focusing on generic reading skills, support children to think about the mental model they have of the specific

(*continued*)

In summary (*continued*)

text they are reading – do they understand what they are reading? Are they supposed to understand?

- The quality of questions used in a classroom is directly linked to the quality of discussion: the best questions are authentic, open-ended and text-specific

- The easiest way for children to develop their vocabulary is through reading widely. Teachers can support vocabulary development through direct teaching of vocabulary, too, including a focus on the most useful words and making children aware of morphology and etymology

- Children's background knowledge is linked to their comprehension. As with vocabulary, it is through wider reading that this will develop, but activating prior knowledge about a specific text and pre-teaching can support understanding too

Bibliography

Beck, I. McKeown, M. and Kucan, L. (2002) *Bringing Words to Life: Robust Vocabulary Instruction*. New York: Guilford Press.

Cain, K., Oakhill, J. V. and Elbro, C. (2003) The ability to learn new word meanings from context by school-age children with and without language comprehension difficulties. *Journal of Child Language*, 30 (3), 681–694.

Cunningham, A. E. (2005) Vocabulary growth through independent reading and reading aloud to children. In E. H. Hiebert & M. L. Kamhi (eds.), *Teaching and learning vocabulary: Bringing research to practice* (pp. 45–68). Mahwah, NJ: Lawrence Erlbaum Associates.

Elleman, A (2017) Examining the impact of inference instruction on the literal and inferential comprehension of skilled an less skilled readers: A meta-analytic review. *Journal of Educational Psychology* 109 (6), 2.

Harrison, C. and Howard, S. (2009) *Inside the Primary Black Box: Assessment for Learning in Primary and Early Years Classrooms*. London: GL Assessment.

Krashen, S. (2004) *The Power of Reading: Insights from the Research*. Westport, CT: Libraries Unlimited.

Tennant, W., Reedy, D., Hobsbaum, A. and Gamble, N. (2016) *Guiding Readers: Layers of Meaning*. London: UCL, Institute of Education.

Literature

A Well-Mannered Young Wolf by Jean Leroy and Mattieu Maudet
Charlotte's Web by E. B. White
Dover Beach by Matthew Arnold
Dulce et Decorum Est by Wilfred Owen
For the Fallen by Laurence Binyon
Good Little Wolf by Nadia Shireen
Goodnight Mr Tom by Michelle Magorian
Julius Caesar by William Shakespeare
Little Red Riding Hood
Montmorency by Eleanor Updale
Shackleton's Journey by William Grill
The Call of the Wild by Jack London
The Wolves of Willoughby Chase by Joan Aiken
Treasure Island by Robert Louis Stevenson
Eagle of the Ninth by Rosemary Sutcliff
What Mr Darwin Saw by Mick Manning

Choosing to read
Building an authentic reading culture

6

Reading is one of the most important things a child can learn at primary school. The ability to read fluently and understand what they read gives children access to new ideas and knowledge, not to mention the lifetime of joy that being a reader can bring. Leaving primary school unable to read makes it very difficult to access the curriculum at secondary school, difficult to access the modern world and difficult for a child to go on to choose what they want to do in later life.

As a result, schools across the world dedicate huge amounts of effort and resources into teaching children to read. But learning *how to* read is only half of the story. If a child learns to read at school, but never chooses to read apart from when they are directed to, then they miss all the benefits that reading widely brings. These include a range of reported academic benefits:

- A correlation between reading engagement and reading attainment (De Naeghel *et al.*, 2012; Morgan and Fuchs, 2007; OECD, 2002, 2010).
- Improved general knowledge (Cunningham and Stanovich, 1998)
- A possible effect on wider academic performance (OECD, 2002)
- Better performance in spelling and mathematics tests (Sullivan and Brown, 2013)
- Improved vocabulary development (Sullivan and Brown, 2013)
- A link between reading and self-confidence in reading (Guthrie and Alvermann, 1999)

- A link to both improved achievement and more positive attitudes to writing (Clark, 2016; Cremin and Myhill, 2012)

Aside from the academic benefits, a child who doesn't read misses out on the pleasure that reading can bring. Whether it is a gripping story, a poem that captures a mood or idea perfectly, a fascinating website or a non-fiction book that provides the answer to a burning question: reading can enrich our lives.

Ideally, children would develop this positive attitude to reading at home, but unfortunately not all children are lucky enough to grow up in a home where reading for pleasure is promoted and modelled. Perhaps this is understandable; children today have many other activities competing for their time. It might be a swimming club, after-school activities, maths tutors or instrument lessons. It might be television and games consoles. Finding free time to read in the busy modern world can be tricky.

If seeing the value to wider reading can't or won't come from home, then it falls to schools that fill that void. Alongside teaching children *how* to read, schools can (and should) play an important part in helping children to *want* to read.

The challenge schools face, with an already packed curriculum, is how to go about this. Despite the well-reported benefits of wider reading, time spent reading is a long-term investment: it doesn't bring immediate results. It takes confidence and foresight to dedicate curriculum time for something as soft-sounding as reading for pleasure at the expense of something more tangible like discrete grammar teaching or comprehension activities. To decide to prioritise building a culture where wider reading is valued takes belief in its importance and a confidence that it will bear fruit in the longer term.

Think and reflect

A problem with the term 'reading for pleasure'?

The term 'reading for pleasure' has become the most common name for the reading that children choose to do voluntarily at

(*continued*)

Think and reflect (*continued*)

home and at school, as opposed to the directed reading of the school curriculum. The term 'reading for pleasure' has been defined as:

> Reading that we do of our own free will, anticipating the satisfaction that we will get from the act of reading. It also refers to reading that having begun at someone else's request we continue because we are interested in it.
>
> (Clark and Rumbold, 2006)

This is an excellent definition of the type of reading we are discussing in this chapter, but it could describe reading for lots of different reasons: reading a non-fiction book to find out about a subject that we find fascinating or reading a horror story and turning the pages out of an awful compulsion to find out what will happen next.

An over-simplification of the term 'reading for pleasure' can sometimes lead to a heavy focus on books that well-meaning adults assume will appeal to children – humorous texts full of cartoon drawings or books that are linked to their immediate interests: football or fairies, perhaps. While there is nothing wrong with children choosing to read and enjoy these books, it can mask the complexity of the reading experience and fail to reflect the full breadth of reasons why people choose to read. Perhaps, as teachers, we need to recognise and share the different emotions that reading can bring about beyond humour and warmth: fascination or sadness, for example. These are equally valid reasons for someone to become lost in a book, even if weeping at the fate of the protagonist or struggling to follow a complicated scientific idea might not always be described as pleasurable. It might be that through promoting a book that inspires a different emotion, a particular child begins to see the value and enjoyment in reading.

Building a genuine reading culture

There is an obvious problem if we try to force children to undertake the 'reading that we do of our own free will' (Clark and Rumbold, 2006). It is impossible to make children read for pleasure. Instead, schools need to create a culture where reading is valued and celebrated, time is made on the curriculum for free voluntary reading and children are introduced to inspiring books. These elements help to create a culture where it is difficult for children not to see the value and enjoyment in reading and where not being a reader is the exception. One model suggests that these 'reading schools':

- Place reading and books at the centre of the curriculum
- Recognise that being able to read well is a key life skill for children, whatever their background
- Believe that every child can learn to read with the right teaching and support
- Acknowledge that not all children will have had the opportunity to develop a love of reading at home, so this has to be taught and encouraged at school – just like any other area of the curriculum
- Build time for all children to read independently, read aloud and be read to during the school day
- Develop a coherent whole-school strategy for promoting reading for pleasure
- Spend money and time to support reading, including buying books and developing the school environment to support reading
- Believe that every teacher should be an advocate for reading
- Devote time to training staff so they are equipped to support children's enjoyment of reading
- Involve parents to ensure the culture of reading that the school has developed extends into the home

(Clements, 2013)

The key to building a genuine reading culture is to ensure that the approaches that promote reading are authentic, rather than merely playing lip service to promoting reading through annual special events or competitions. This might be considered through:

Staff

The quality and consistency of teaching at a school is one of the key factors that can affect children's progress in reading. If we want a generation of children who enjoy reading, it is vital that they learn to read well, developing fluent word-reading and sophisticated comprehension skills, as we have seen in Chapter 4. Cremin *et al.* (2009) suggest that school staff can play a more important part than simply teaching the mechanics of reading, instead helping to develop children's positive attitudes to reading. Some practical approaches for promoting reading might include:

Time to talk about books – reading is often a personal activity; something that is done independently. We can help children to become keener readers through opportunities to talk about texts and build a shared understanding. This might be through whole class discussion, through small-group reading or through children reading the same book independently and then having time to talk. Children need an opportunity to compare ideas and argue about the books they have read. One of the benefits of rich texts is that there is often ambiguity with characters and the dilemmas they face and themes and ideas that great books can introduce. This gives children plenty to talk about.

Staff sharing their reading experiences – for many children, the adults they see every day at school will be the most regular reading role models in their life. If staff can talk passionately about reading, share their opinions (and listen to the opinions of children) and talk about the books (and other texts) they read, this can help reading to be both valuable (an activity worth doing) and also normal (an activity that people choose to do every day). This might be through formal approaches, such as assemblies where books are shared, 'what I'm reading' displays on classroom doors or through events such as World Book Day. But it can also happen through the unplanned day-to-day conversations that adults have with children. Often it is these that are most valuable for promoting reading in an authentic way.

Staff being knowledgeable about children's books – having a good knowledge of children's literature, both classic and contemporary, is important for teachers if they are going to be role models for reading. A good and current knowledge enables them to choose books for specific purposes: reading aloud or illustrating a specific teaching point. It also allows them to make recommendations of books that specific children might be interested in. Regularly browsing bookshops, reading some of the many blogs and websites about children's books and looking at the long and shortlists for children's book awards, such as the Carnegie Award, the Greenaway Award or the UKLA Children's Book Award, are all great places to start.

Why not try?

A quick search online will reveal a great many lists of 'top children's books' compiled by websites or newspapers each year. The trouble is that these booklists often feature the same 'classics' or are heavily dominated by the same authors. One useful approach is to create a school booklist – everyone in the school, from the youngest children to the staff and parents, share their favourite books, which are then complied into a list. Not only does the process result in an up-to-date booklist that can be shared on the school's website, it also gives everyone the chance to talk about their favourite books, raising the profile of reading in the school.

Curriculum

The school curriculum has sometimes been seen as a barrier to children enjoying reading, with the need for children to reach centrally-imposed standards in reading and certain teaching practices promoted by the Primary National Strategy running counter to developing children's wider reading for pleasure (Lockwood, 2008). If the curriculum is carefully planned, with texts chosen to appeal to and challenge children, there is no reason why the teaching of reading at school should work in opposition to reading for pleasure. The key message of this book is that a text-based approach to teaching can support children to become more confident readers and writers, but also can help them to develop a positive attitude to reading and writing. As a result, Chapters 2 and 3 consider the curriculum in detail, but some practical strategies a school can adopt are:

Adopting a text-based curriculum – through the process of reading, thinking about and discussing books and poems, children have the opportunity to encounter a wide range of different texts. These texts, which might be studied over a long period of time, can come to be the books that children form the strongest bonds with. Crucial to an effective text-based curriculum that is designed to maximise enjoyment of reading as well as raising attainment is the time to read whole texts, rather than simply a series of extracts, and the time to listen to parts of the story without a specific educational focus or teaching point. While sometimes it is important to analyse a text in order to make a teaching point, sometimes it is equally important to share the story and reflect on it as a reader, rather than as a scholar. This way of thinking might help to avoid 'death by analysis', a certain way of killing any enjoyment that might come from reading.

Independent reading – independent reading at school for a sustained period of time is an important way of helping children to develop as self-reliant readers – able to select a book and maintain concentration. Independent reading is an equitable activity because it means that every child, including those who do not read at home, have time to enjoy a book every day. Independent reading works best if there is also an opportunity for children to talk about the books they are reading. Depending on the age of the children and the experiences they have from the rest of the curriculum, children may have their choice of text guided by the teacher or have a free choice in what they read.

Reading aloud – reading aloud provides an opportunity for children to share the enjoyment of a text together, making reading into a communal activity. Aside from the educational benefits, including comprehension and vocabulary development, sharing a book aloud can be a joyful time of day where children have the opportunity to see the pleasure in books and reading.

Think and reflect

Reading schools plan their curriculum carefully, looking critically at what they do. Three questions to ask are:

- Is this activity making a child better at reading or helping them to develop a positive attitude to reading?
- Is this activity as effective as it could be in its purpose?
- Is there a clear rationale to what the children are doing?

If not, then changes to that aspect of the curriculum might need to be made. Children are at school for such a short amount of time, that if we are going to support them to become confident and keen readers, every bit of the school day has to earn its place.

Although it is rarely commented on, one of the most significant changes in the 2014 National Curriculum is the addition of reading for pleasure:

> Pupils should be taught to read fluently, understand extended prose, both fiction and non-fiction, and be encouraged to read for pleasure. Schools should do everything to promote wider reading . . . [Pupils] should be reading widely and frequently, outside as well as in school, for pleasure and information.
>
> *(DfE, 2013)*

For schools following the English curriculum, this provides a welcome spur for a focus on reading for pleasure and children's wider reading.

Physical environment

The reading environment in a school encompasses far more than the physical spaces where books are stored and displayed and where children can read. This might include the choice of books, time given over to reading, mood of the reader and purpose for reading – 'the social context of reading' (Chambers, 1993). However, the physical environment of a school can play a positive part in helping children choose to read. This might include spaces for reading, book areas, book corners and displays about books and reading. While the physical environment might be attractive and welcoming, the most important element is that the reading environment provides working spaces that are organised for reading. An attractive display may make the books look more appealing, but the range of texts available and the time to browse, choose and read them is likely to be a more significant factor on children's reading in the long run.

Links with home

Involving families in building a reading culture is vital. International reading studies have shown children who are supported in their reading at home are much more likely to enjoy reading and tend to achieve more highly at school and that the effect of parents being involved at primary school lasts throughout a child's school years and can still be seen at the age of 15 (OECD, 2012). The aim is for schools to harness the enthusiasm of families by providing guidance, advice and resources to make reading at home as easy, enjoyable and fruitful as it can be. For the small number of families who may find it more difficult to engage with their children's learning, schools need to offer support in a non-threatening way. And for those families who can't or won't support their child's reading, schools need to compensate for this, ensuring that a child who doesn't access to books and reading at home still has the opportunity to see reading as a positive activity.

Regular communication throughout a child's time at school –
there is often a great deal of contact with parents in the early years of
school, with parents invited in to for presentations about early reading and about the importance of reading with their child. This is
supported through the books that are sent home being changed regularly and notes in reading diaries. As children move through the
school, and their reading becomes more independent, opportunities
to communicate with parents can become less frequent. Making time
to share the importance of regular reading with parents and their
children can help this important activity to continue, helping the
support from home to complement the teaching that happens in
school. This might be through regular meetings, reminders in news-
letters or text updates, or it might be through informal chats in the
playground. Every school will have its own ways of contacting
parents, but what is important is that parents and schools are working
together towards the same end.

Reading diaries – at their best, reading diaries can be an important
tool for communication between home and school, allowing children's
reading experiences to be captured and shared. For older children,
reading diaries can be a way of reflecting on the books that they have
read. But in practice, reading diaries can also be problematic. For some
families, filling a reading diary can be a challenge – this might be because
of difficulties with literacy or language or it might be for organisational
reasons. Either way, the dialogue about reading between home and
school can shift from being one about the benefits of reading and the
enjoyment it can bring to a conversation about why a diary hasn't been
signed. This can get in the way of productive conversations. With older
children, where they complete their own diaries, it can add a chore,
'some work' after the enjoyable act of reading. For some children,
responding in writing each time they read effectively becomes a punish-
ment for reading.

Every school will use reading diaries differently, and in many schools
they are a valuable way of celebrating reading and establishing a link
between home and school. However, as with everything in schools,
there is no compulsion to use them. If they are not helping a child to

become a better reader or helping them to see the value in reading, then their use needs to be questioned, especially if they are taking parents' or teachers' time away from other more valuable activities.

Reading initiatives and celebrations

The key to building a genuine reading culture is to ensure that the approaches that promote reading are authentic, rather than being undertaken for appearance. Special events that celebrate or promote reading, sometimes by dressing up, can play an important part in raising the profile of books and reading. They can also be a lot of fun, which can be an outcome in itself – there is nothing wrong with fun at school. As a celebration of a school's rich reading culture, special events can be valuable, but they are unlikely to work on their own. Events to raise the profile of reading often work best when they have been planned for a specific purpose or to address a particular issue.

From reading competitions to extreme reading displays to DEAR time, there are many popular ways of promoting reading in schools. As with everything, the challenge is to make them as authentic as possible, so the focus is on reading and books, rather than an activity which might be exciting initially, but then fail to have lasting results.

Reading competitions

Individual reading competitions can be very motivating, but setting children against each other doesn't help to build a class into a community of readers. Instead, a team-challenge takes the best elements of a competition, but encourages children to work together. Some good whole-school challenges might be:

Reading challenge – as a class, read all of one author's books in a week – you can plan which classes or children will read which book, sharing them out amongst the children. Then the children can get started, filling every spare moment with reading until they are done.

Read to the Pole – use a map app to calculate how far it is from your school to the North Pole. Set the whole school the challenge of reading a book for every mile and count how long it takes you for to read them and reach your goal. Different classes could compete to see who has contributed the most miles.

Reading Buddies

Many schools use a system of reading buddies, where older children meet with a younger child to share a book or hear them read. The younger children benefit from the opportunity to read aloud to someone who they look up to. But the partnership can also benefit the older child who has the responsibility of being the expert and supporting someone else's reading. This can help them to be conscious about what makes a good reader and can have an impact on their own reading, especially if they are reading aloud to another child.

Rewarding reading

Extrinsic rewards for reading such as stickers, bookmarks or points on a chart can be initially motivating, but they are only valuable if they lead to children forming a reading habit and if children choose to read when they are not on offer. Research suggests that rewarding behaviours with an extrinsic prize can lead to a lack of motivation when the reward is not on offer (Deci *et al.*, 1999). What if this is true of reading?

Drop Everything And Read time

DEAR time is where, at a set time, a class or indeed the whole school stop the activity they are doing and read together. Often the adults stop and read at the same time. The signal could be a bell ringing across the school. This might be a regular occurrence (weekly, perhaps) or on a special occasion such as World Book Day. While time to read a book of their choice for a sustained period is one of the most valuable opportunities we can give children in primary school, DEAR time organised in this way doesn't reflect most people's real reading behaviour. Most adults are not lucky enough to be able to suddenly stop whatever they are doing and settle down to read. Reading time is far more likely to be an activity that is planned into the day: reading on a commute to work or just before bed.

A more authentic approach might be to simply ring-fence regular time for children to read independently. This could be curriculum time each day (first thing in the morning or straight after lunch) or it could be as part of an element of the curriculum, for example during small-group reading where the child is not working in a group with an adult.

As for the teacher using the time to read, while it could be argued that this is them modelling reading, a question has to be asked about whether this is the best way to do this and whether their time could be spent more effectively supporting a child's reading or a listening to a child read. A teacher can share their reading life and be a model for reading by talking about the books that they read and the preferences they have, rather than sitting and reading in front of the children.

Of course DEAR time might be used to make a specific point about the importance of reading, but if we want to give children an authentic independent reading experience, then there may be better ways to go about it.

'Extreme reading' displays

'Extreme reading' is where children (and staff) are photographed reading in an unusual place, such as on ski lift on holiday or buried up to their neck in sand. While these make for an interesting display, they do not represent a terribly authentic reading situation. The trouble is, like DEAR time, they don't reflect real reading. It might be more effective to display:

'Did you enjoy ... ? You might like ... ' – Displays of recommended books, if updated regularly, can be engaging and attractive. They might focus on a specific author or genre, or create a family tree of reading, linking authors with similar styles or themes to broaden children's reading palate.

Children and adults from across the school sharing their favourite book – this might be as a display on a wall or in digital photo frames. While simple, this is valuable as it involves a discussion in order to choose a favourite book and a wall of exciting books and smiling faces can make for an attractive display.

Digital displays – displays about reading can be useful, but once they have been up on a wall for a while, they fade into the background and children stop noticing them. Technology provides a useful way of keeping displays fresh and updated. This could be digital photo frames displaying recommended reads in book corners or a screen saver on interactive whiteboards (IWBs) or other shared screens, sharing book covers, favourite quotes from books or short one-sentence book reviews.

Think and reflect

Four questions to ask before organising a reading initiative might be:

1. Is the initiative actually about reading? Will it help children to become better readers or help them to see the enjoyment in reading?

2. Is it equitable? Can all children access the initiative to the same degree? Events that involve dressing up or contributing money can be difficult for some families

3. Does it help children to see the intrinsic value and enjoyment in reading? Collecting stickers, rewards and points can be very motivating, but are only valuable if children still choose to read when they are not on offer

4. Is there likely to be any lasting effect on reading for the school beyond the actual initiative? Is the amount of effort expended on the event worth it in terms of the impact on children's reading?

Being a reader is about two interrelated aspects: being able to read well and having the desire to read. Thankfully, these two aspects are closely related and support one another. If schools and teachers can adopt an authentic approach to promoting reading, then that will have an impact on children's achievement in reading, bringing them success at primary school and setting them up for later in life. One benefit is the impact that reading widely can have on children's writing: the topic of the next section of this book.

In summary

- There is a strong correlation between children reading widely in their own time and a range of positive educational outcomes
- Reading can also be an enjoyable activity in itself; undertaken not for an educational benefit, but for its own inherent value
- The reasons children might choose to read extend beyond a simplistic notion of pleasure – instantly enjoying a book because it is about their immediate interests or because it is amusing – instead reading for pleasure should acknowledge the many reasons people read, including because they are interested in a subject or because of the range of different emotions that reading can trigger
- If children have not had the chance to see the value of books at home, it is vital that school does everything it can to fill this vacuum
- While special events and competitions can help to create a buzz about reading, it is likely that the ongoing factors of a curriculum that gives children the chance to encounter great books and a staff team who inspire children to read will have a greater impact on children's attitudes to reading in the long term

Bibliography

Chambers, A. (1993) *Tell Me: Children, Reading and Talk*. Stroud: The Thimble Press.

Clark, C. (2016) *Children's and Young People's Reading in 2015. Findings from the 2015 National Literacy Trust's Annual Survey.* London: National Literacy Trust.

Clark C. and Rumbold, K. (2006) *Reading for Pleasure: A Research Overview.* London: National Literacy Trust.

Clements, J. (2013) *Building an Outstanding Reading School.* Oxford: Oxford University Press.

Cremin, T. and Myhill, D. (2012) *Writing Voices: Creating Communities of Writers.* London: Routledge

Cremin, T., Mottram, M., Collins, F., Powell, S. and Safford, K. (2009) Teachers as readers: building communities of readers, *Literacy,* 43 (1) 11–19.

Cunningham, A. and Stanovich, K. (1998) What reading does for the mind. *American Educator,* 22 (1 and 2), 8–15.

De Naeghel, J., Van Keer, H., Vansteenkiste, M., and Rosseel, Y. (2012). The relation between elementary students' recreational and academic reading motivation, reading frequency, engagement, and comprehension: a self-determination theory perspective. *Journal of Educational Psychology,* 104 (3), 1006–1021.

Deci, E. L., Koestner, R., & Ryan, R. M. (1999). A meta-analytic review of experiments examining the effects of extrinsic rewards on intrinsic motivation. *Psychological Bulletin,* 125 (6), 627–668.

DfE (2013) *National Curriculum in England: Primary Curriculum.* London: DfE

Guthrie, J. T. and Alvermann, D. E. (1999) *Engaged Reading: Processes, Practices, and Policy Implications.* New York: Teachers College Press.

Lockwood, M. (2008) *Promoting Reading for Pleasure in the Primary School.* London: SAGE.

Morgan, P. L. and Fuchs, D. (2007). Is there a bidirectional relationship between children's reading skills and reading motivation? *Exceptional Children,* 73 (2), 165–183.

OECD (2002) *Reading for Change: Performance and Engagement Across Countries: Results From PISA 2002.* New York: Organisation for Economic Co-operation and Development.

OECD (2010) *PISA 2009 Results: Learning to Learn-Student Engagement, Strategies and Practices,* Vol. Ill. New York: Organisation for Economic Co-operation and Development.

OECD (2012) *PISA – Let's Read Them a Story! The Parent Factor in Education.* New York: PISA. OECD.

Sullivan, A. and Brown, M. (2013) *Social Inequalities in Cognitive Scores at Age 16: The Role of Reading.* CLS Working Paper 2013/10. London: Centre for Longitudinal Studies.

PART 3

Teaching writing by the book

A model for teaching writing

The ability to express their thoughts clearly in writing is a crucial skill for children to develop in primary school. Without it, it's very difficult for children to go on and achieve academic success. A child might have the most wonderful understanding of science or history, but if they can't express that knowledge and understanding in writing, the chances are that their expertise won't be recognised. But good writing is more important than that. The ability to write well gives people power – the power to entertain, to delight, to enlighten or to persuade. Writing is about communication. Helping children to learn to control language to communicate exactly what they want to say is a gift that will give a child a voice that others will listen to.

So how can we best support children to develop strong writing skills at primary school? Certainly, part of the answer lies in using rich texts to model and stimulate the writing children do. This chapter will consider some effective approaches to teaching writing in primary school, suggesting key principles for teaching writing in primary school.

Genres, text types and writing

The dominant model for teaching writing in primary schools in England for more than a decade has been that of text types or genres, embedded in many classrooms through the National Primary Strategy (DfES, 2006), and before that, the National Literacy Strategy (DfES, 1999). At the heart of this model is the idea that there are specific genres of writing, each with a clearly defined set of features and language structures. If children can learn to recognise and employ the features of each of these genres, they will become effective writers. The academic view of genre is broader and more sophisticated than that which has found its way into schools: recognising that genres are social constructs for communicating ideas and knowledge and that they are liable to change and look different depending on context and use, rather than being one fixed set of conventions for a different purpose (Swales, 1990; Freedman and Medway, 1994). This is reflected in the writing children do in the real world, which often fails to sit within one of the Primary Strategy's tidy genres. As Myhill and Fisher (2010) note:

> as writers develop, they have to learn not simply about formulaic patterns of text types but how genres are socially situated and mediated by their context.

There are certainly benefits to approaching teaching writing in this way: a focus on genres allows children to understand the purpose of a text and provide a frame on which to hang their own writing, learning about the different language features, both grammatical and structural. However, this can lead to a very rigid way of teaching children to write – one that often makes heavy use of success criteria to scaffold children's writing and where children's writing is seen as being right or wrong when compared to the features of a specific text type, rather than being evaluated against the intended purpose of the writing. It can also promote a deficit model of teaching writing, where the expectation is that children arrive in the classroom with little knowledge of how to communicate. This ignores their existing knowledge drawn from the texts they read and language they encounter every day. This view of writing as an incremental series of skills to be acquired has been reinforced by commercial writing schemes that suggest there is a set formula for good writing that involves the rigid use of certain language features and vocabulary boiled down to an acronym. If we want children to become craftsmen with words, then we need to move beyond this mechanistic approach to teaching writing.

The 2014 National Curriculum in England makes no mention of different genres of writing, instead stating that children should learn to: 'write clearly, accurately and coherently, adapting their language and style in and for a range of contexts, purposes and audiences' (DfE, 2013).

In many classrooms this was always the case, with skilled teachers bringing the text types to life by giving children real purposes to write, or making links to the wider curriculum or to the books they read together. An approach to teaching writing based on text types doesn't necessarily need to be in conflict with an approach that is based on audience and purpose: the text type that children are writing might well provide the purpose for writing. But, if we want to create a generation of children who are flexible and creative in their written communication, the ability to tailor their writing for their audience and purpose needs to come before adhering to a set of tight success criteria for a particular text type.

Teaching sequence

The approach to organising text-based units of work that is advocated in this book owes much to the integrated model of planning first outlined in *Raising Boys' Achievement in Writing* (2004). The three-phase model will be familiar with many primary teachers through the old Primary Strategy (both the genre-based units and additional text-based units):

- Phase 1 – familiarisation with the genre
- Phase 2 – capturing ideas and planning
- Phase 3 – writing and presenting

The phases are organised so that children:

> ... become confidently *familiar* with the features of the chosen text type. Ideas for writing will be *captured* in a variety of ways, but this part of the process is where the class is likely to benefit from talk, drama or role play activities which will support their grasp of the whole text structure (for example, role play to aid personal narrative or persuasive argument). Writing in many forms may be

part of the process from the start, but once there has been extensive experience of the text features, the process of teacher *demonstrating,* modelling and guiding writing is used to *support* successful sustained and *independent* writing.

(UKLA/PNS, 2004)

It has proven to be an influential model and remains a popular structure for organising units of work in English. A text-based approach to English teaching presents several challenges if we wish to work with this successful framework.

The first challenge is that the texts used to drive a unit have not necessarily been chosen because they will familiarise children with a specific genre. The text *might* provide a direct model for what a child is expected to write, but it might also be a very different type of text chosen as a stimulus for writing instead (for example, a newspaper report based on events in a piece of narrative fiction). The second challenge is that when working with a longer text, such as a novel or play, the initial phase of familiarisation could take a long time. It would be difficult (and probably undesirable) to read the entire text before moving on to the planning and creating phases.

An additional challenge to teachers in English schools is the approach to teaching writing advocated by the 2014 National Curriculum: plan, draft and evaluate-edit/redraft, which must be integrated with this model (DfE, 2013). A process which puts greater emphasis on editing and redrafting gives teachers an opportunity to show some of the skills of writing at a different point in the teaching sequence. The final challenge to the three-phase model is that if a teacher sticks rigidly to units that build to piece of writing every three weeks, children might only write two extended pieces of writing each half term. If children are going to become accomplished writers, it will help for them to write more often than this.

The answer to these challenges might be to employ a slightly more flexible approach which keeps to the spirit of each phase, but doesn't organise these phases into a rigid linear sequence. Instead of the unit moving through three phases sequentially, there is the opportunity for children to work through the three phases a number of times within the unit. This change in structure means that children do not get a long phase of familiarisation, but they will still have an opportunity to explore the genre, thinking about their audience and purpose before they write. This model also takes into account children's previous learning and experience. If children in Year Four are creating a piece of instructional writing, then it is very likely they will have written instructions before. Most shouldn't need a full introduction to the genre as if they were starting from scratch. Instead, a reminder (considering the audience and purpose for writing) about the text they are going to write should be enough for most children. An increased focus on evaluating and editing means they'll have the opportunity to develop and improve their writing later in the process. While a unit may have an extended familiarisation stage, this is as likely to be concerned with familiarisation with the text, the story, characters, themes or ideas, as it is with later writing demands. Appendix II, explored in Chapter 4, gives a unit of work for *The Labours of Hercules* that follows this model.

Think and reflect

Think about the model of teaching writing that is followed in your school or classroom:

- Does it allow children to think carefully about their intended audience and purpose when they write?
- Is there the flexibility for children to create pieces of writing that sit between the fixed genres of the old Literacy Strategy?

Factors for teaching writing effectively

An effective model for teaching writing might be built on several key principles:

1. Support children to see themselves as writers
2. Encourage children to think about writing as a process

3. Teach children to write by emulating great writing
4. Enable children to improve their writing through feedback
5. Acknowledge that writing can be hard

Support children to see themselves as writers

Helping children to see themselves as writers, rather than 'someone who does some writing when they're told to' is a crucial element in teaching writing. If we can encourage children to see themselves as writers – someone who shapes words and language to create a particular effect – then not only are they more likely to write well, but they are likely to be motivated to want to improve their writing. If children are writing for us, their teachers, because they have to, then the responsibility for improving lies with us to cajole them into becoming better. If they are writing for themselves because they see themselves as a writer, then they are far more likely to want to learn to control the language they use. Above all, we want children to become craftsmen with language. As teacher and author Ron Berger writes:

> Craftsman. This one word says it all. It connotes someone who has integrity and knowledge, who is dedicated to his work and is proud of what he does and who he is. Someone who thinks carefully and does things well. I want a classroom full of craftsmen. I want students whose work is strong and accurate and beautiful. Students who are proud of what they do, proud of how they respect both themselves and others.
>
> (Berger, 2003)

Encourage children to think about writing as a process

For some children, writing is all about the end product. For them, writing is a noun – a thing – rather than a process. If we want children to become writers who are able to reflect on their work, seeking to refine the words and language they use, then we have to persuade them that the piece of writing isn't finished once their pencil adds a full stop after the final word. A strong model for the teaching of writing is built on the idea that once the first draft is complete the real work of writing can start. The 2014 National Curriculum (DfE, 2013) suggests a four-step framework for the writing process:

Plan – collecting ideas and mapping out the piece of writing

Draft – writing the first draft following their plan, but deviating from it where they have a better idea

Evaluate – considering the strengths and weaknesses the first draft

Edit/redraft – an opportunity for children to make improvements to their first draft in the light of the evaluation stage

While these stages provide a useful way of thinking about how a child might move through the writing process, they could lead to an approach to writing that is overly procedural. Real writing is unlikely to neatly follow this linear route every time.

What is important is that the spirit of the steps is followed, with children having the chance to think about what they write, create a draft and then refine that draft in the light of feedback, rather than following the same structure every time they write. The emphasis given to each of these stages will depend on the purpose of the writing and the expected outcome. Writing notes ready for a discussion in class might not need much in the way of planning, but they will certainly benefit from being evaluated and proofread before they are used. A piece of non-fiction writing linked to history lessons might be planned carefully, ensuring that the key information is organised and appropriate vocabulary is employed. A story might follow all the stages, even if the final outcome is very different from the initial plan. By explicitly teaching children how to approach each of these stages, we are teaching them to hone a piece of writing until it says exactly what they want it to say: a key attribute of an effective writer (Bereiter and Scardamalia, 1987).

Children should learn to write by emulating great writing

One of the best ways of learning to write is by studying how real authors use words and language to communicate. Giving children the opportunity to analyse high-quality texts, both classic and contemporary, means they can see how language is used for specific effects. A good teacher of writing draws children's attention to the level of individual words, phrases, punctuation and grammar, as well as the broad themes and ideas in the text. Children are given the opportunity to consider how the author has made conscious choices about the content and style of the text. This is where a text-based method of teaching English comes into its own. We want to see how an author communicates their thoughts and ideas to a particular audience.

Texts might be used as stimuli for writing, as a direct model for language or structure or there may be a looser link, with the books that child has read being 'absorbed' through reading and then being used unconsciously in a child's writing (Barrs and Cork, 2001). This idea forms the basis of Chapter 8.

Feedback enables children to improve their writing

Effective feedback, both oral and written, is how children learn to be better writers. Meaningful, formative feedback should be focused on improving children's work, giving children clear advice on how to improve. Oral feedback might be delivered through simple prompts, suggestions and advice or through questions to make a child think about their writing. Children then need time to act on the feedback and make changes to their work. An effective feedback process will look different in every classroom, but some ideas to try might be:

1. **A chance to proofread independently** – the first stage of feedback is to give the child some time to try to identify where there are mistakes or where they could make improvements. The point of this checking time is to ensure that the children can self-correct the little errors that often slip into their writing if they are producing an

extended piece. If a teacher marks a child's first draft, the chances are they'll end up correcting secretarial mistakes, rather than the other aspects that will improve their writing. It's very possible that the child has made mistakes through rushing to finish. If children are taught to use this time to check their work, it means that any mistakes after this are likely to be conceptual errors that need to be taught, rather than mistakes that children have made through carelessness or rushing. This enables the teacher to use her limited time to teach the things that will have the greatest impact on children's development in writing. Generally, the older children are, the easier they find this task, but if younger children can make even one improvement then this stage has been worthwhile as it helps them to learn to become a more autonomous learner. To help, children can be taught to read their writing aloud, making sure they read each word as it's written.

2. **Reading the children's initial drafts** – in the next stage, the teacher takes in the whole class' written work and reads it, making brief notes on what individual children need to do in order to develop their writing. They also note down any common misconceptions or recurring errors to inform the whole-class teaching. Children's initial drafts could be copied and kept as a record of children's level of achievement in writing when working independently, useful for making summative assessments of standards in writing. Having a copy (either photocopied or as a photograph), means the children can make changes to their original draft, rather than having to write it out again.

3. **Teaching points for the whole class** – From looking briefly at the children's writing, the teacher begins the session by sharing the areas many of the class members would benefit from learning about. These might be an aspect of grammar or punctuation or a focus on composition, such as techniques for descriptions or effective dialogue. These may be taught as a discrete session or be drawn out through sharing a child's work for editing using a visualizer or IWB. Looking at key areas to improve for the class as a whole can be an excellent way of teaching writing skills in a context that makes

them meaningful for children. Using children's work as examples (in a supportive and sensitive manner) sends a clear message that every piece of work in the room can be improved. It can also provide motivation for children to gain an understanding of specific aspects of English. Once they have learnt how to do something, they are more likely to be motivated to change them in their own work, improving what they have written.

4. **Individual oral feedback** – the next step in the process is some immediate oral feedback. The teacher holds each piece of work up and suggests one or two things that the child should look at to improve their work. This might be organised by the teacher working around the classroom spending a few moments with each child or through working with groups (in guided writing, perhaps). With older children, this oral feedback could be done in front of the whole class (in a supportive and sensitive manner), so everyone benefits from hearing the feedback. Children then have time to improve their writing in the light of this feedback.

5. **Extended written or oral feedback** – to be as effective as possible, feedback needs to be diagnostic, clear and focussed on how each child can improve their writing. The best written feedback will focus on just a few key areas to address, often phrased as targets, action points of things to change or as questions to prompt thinking and reflection. If the writing needs more than this to move it to a good standard, then it might well be a better use of time to work through the piece with the child, providing oral feedback and rectifying errors together. Providing detailed written feedback can be very time-consuming, but it can have an impact on the quality of children's writing and what they learn in a session. However, this is only true if children have the opportunity to act on the teacher's advice. Time spent marking children's work should happen before children have written their final draft – children can then show that they have learnt from it by making changes in their final draft. With younger children, a guided writing session, with the teacher sitting and working on the writing with the child, might be more effective than marking their work. This potentially time-consuming approach

might not be possible all of the time, but it's one of the best ways of improving children's writing.

A model of feedback such as this shifts responsibility for improving the writing to the child, reflecting the aim of helping a child to become a self-motivated writer, keen to improve and develop, rather than being a passive participant waiting to be told what they can do to improve.

Think and reflect

To what extent do you agree with the following statements about marking and feedback? How well do they match with the process of marking in your school or classroom?

- Feedback should validate what children have done well already
- The best feedback often comes in the middle of the writing process, so children have the opportunity to act on it and improve their work
- Building in time to self-check helps children to become autonomous and take responsibility for their own writing
- Ongoing assessments should feed back into teaching. Rather than teaching to a predetermined plan, a good teacher adapts the lesson to support children's learning
- Using children's work as examples (in a sensitive way) sends a clear message that every piece of work in the room can be improved

The most important aspect of any feedback is that, to make it meaningful, the children have the opportunity to act on it and use it to improve their writing. This is why feedback is probably most useful at the draft stage, when the class have an opportunity to edit or redraft their work in the light of assessment.

Acknowledge that writing can be hard

Sometimes writing is easy: the ideas flow and the text seems to write itself, but very often it is a difficult process and finding the right words to express an idea is a puzzle that needs to be solved. To create an accomplished piece of writing, there are many different elements for children to consider and control:

- The audience and purpose of writing
- The ideas they wish to convey
- The structure and cohesion of the text
- Vocabulary
- Grammar
- Spelling
- Punctuation
- Handwriting or typing

Balancing these demands can be a challenge for children's working memory, stretching the limits of children's processing power when trying to balance them all (Myhill and Fisher, 2010). More than anything, writing is hard because communicating exactly what you mean involves thinking clearly and that is very tricky indeed.

It is important that teachers acknowledge that writing can be hard, but also that there is a reward for persisting until we find a solution. As teachers, we need to share the message that the best writers don't necessarily find writing easy, instead they enjoy the fact that it is hard. This idea of struggling at something and then slowly, through effort and thought, reaching an answer should sit at the heart of how we teach writing. If children are finding it easy every time that they write, it is very possible that they should be undertaking a more challenging task. Making a link between effort, practice and improvement can be difficult: few things are valued as highly in modern culture as effort-less achievement – the ability to be successful without trying (Eyre, 2011). Helping children to see the link between their effort and the outcomes is vital and further supports the need to encourage children to see themselves as writers, striving to become better at communicating through written language.

Think and reflect

Thinking about your school or classroom:
- Are children encouraged to undertake challenging writing tasks?
- Are they allowed to sometimes struggle with difficult concepts?
- Do they have the opportunity to keep trying until they solve the puzzle?

In Chapter 3, we considered how this approach to teaching writing can be combined with reading to create meaningful units of work for English. In the next chapter, we'll look at some practical ways that great books can support the development of children's writing.

In summary

- While learning to write using specific genres or text types can provide a useful scaffold for children, it can be restrictive and does not always reflect the writing that happens in the real world
- A broad teaching sequence for writing that allows for familiarisation with a text, capturing ideas, planning and then writing and presenting is vital, but some flexibility within this structure is desirable so that children have opportunities to write regularly and can write on occasions without scaffolds in place

(continued)

In summary (*continued*)

● Five key aspects of teaching writing effectively are:

1. Support children to see themselves as writers
2. Encourage children to think about writing as a process
3. Teach children to write by emulating great writing
4. Enable children to improve their writing through feedback
5. Acknowledge that writing can be hard

And these should inform the pedagogy of and planning for writing in primary schools. Teaching children to think of themselves as a writer, thinking about writing as a process and using feedback effectively all shift responsibility for writing onto the child, rather than the teacher.

Bibliography

Barrs, M. and Cork, V. (2001) *The Reader in the Writer*. London: Centre for Language in Primary Education.

Bereiter, C. and Scardamalia, M. (1987) *The Psychology of Written Composition*. Hillsdale. New Jersey: Lawrence Erlbaum.

Berger, R. (2003) *An Ethic of Excellence: Building a Culture of Craftsmanship with Students*. Portsmouth, NH: Heinemann.

DfE (2013) *National Curriculum in England: Primary Curriculum*. London: DfE.

DfES (1999) *National Literacy Strategy*. London: DfES.

DfES (2006) *Primary National Strategy – A Framework for Literacy*. London: DfES.

Eyre, D. (2011) *Room at the Top: Inclusive Education for High Performance*. London: Policy Exchange.

Freedman, A. and Medway, P. (eds) (1994) *Genre and the New Rhetoric*. London: Taylor and Francis.

Myhill, D. and Fisher, R. (2010) Editorial: Writing development: cognitive, sociocultural, linguistic perspectives. *Journal of Research in Reading*, 33 (1), 1–3.

Swales, J. (1990) *Genre Analysis.* Cambridge: Cambridge University Press.

UKLA/Primary National Strategy (2004) *Raising Boys' Achievement in Writing.* Leicester: UKLA.

Literature

The Labours of Hercules

Teaching writing

Learning to be a writer

There are many different sources of inspiration for writing – real life events (both organised in school and children's own experiences), films and other multi-media texts, drama and educational visits or visitors to school, not to mention a child's own imagination. A rich English curriculum draws on all of these to motivate and inspire children to write. A great text can also be a powerful starting point for writing, offering both a stimulus and a model for mature and confident writing. This chapter will look at some practical ways that a text-based approach to teaching can help children to become confident and creative writers.

You are what you read

The books that children read, with patterns of language so different from those of spoken language, give children the building blocks of words, phrases, structural devices and ideas with which to be creative in their own writing.

While we might not know a great deal about *how* reading informs writing, teachers' classroom experiences of working with young writers suggests that the two are closely linked (Dockrell and Connelly, 2009). Research appears to confirm this, recognising a relationship between achievement in reading and writing (Barrs and Cork, 2001). Professional authors are often quick to cite the impact of their reading on their writing. As Stephen King notes in his excellent book *On Writing*:

> If you want to be a writer, you must do two things above all others: read a lot and write a lot. There's no way around these two things that I'm aware of, no shortcut.
>
> (King, 2012)

There are two ways teachers can help children to absorb the ideas and linguistic patterns from great books, and we can crudely divide those into those that are *taught* and those that are *caught*.

Reading into writing – caught

This is the natural process of children soaking up language and ideas as they read. As we've seen already in Chapter 6, independent reading – reading for pleasure – can have a profound impact on a child's wider education. While all independent reading is likely to support children's writing (as well as hopefully being a source of enjoyment and entertainment), there are three factors to think about with regard to the texts that might best support writing development.

Quantity – simply put, the more that children read, the greater chance they have to encounter and absorb new language and new ideas. Anything we can do to give children more time to read, whether that is at home or at school, is likely to support them to become better writers. The effects of this might not be seen immediately and it could take years for the results of the reading they do to filter through into their writing, but adopting this longer-term view is valuable nonetheless.

Quality – as we've seen this is a potentially tricky concept as any judgement about the quality of a text will be subjective. The key thing about independent, self-directed reading is that the reader has a choice in what they read, rather than being pushed towards a text that will better them or be good for their writing. However, we have a duty as teachers to broaden children's horizons and introduce them to books they might not pick up otherwise, and if we can support children to find wonderful, rich texts that will extend their thinking and introduce them to new language, then so much the better.

Range – there's nothing wrong with having a favourite author or enjoying all of the books in a particular series, but if children read just one type of work they miss out on the breadth of different styles and ideas. A child who only reads non-fiction may find himself struggling to write an exciting short story. Another who favours one particular author to the exclusion of all others may find herself adopting the language structures, narrative style and preoccupations of their favourite books. Teachers sometimes bemoan children's lack of imagination, but instead it may be that they don't have the reservoir of language and ideas needed to develop a confident writing voice.

Perhaps none of these things are as important as the fact that a child is reading at all, but the greater the quantity, quality and range of a child's reading, the greater the range of language they will have to draw on as a writer. Developing these three qualities in children's reading is a matter of equity. Many children will listen to and read a range of books as they grow up. They might be lucky enough to live in a house full of books or be enthusiastic members of the local library. They might have a parent who reads to them every night or tells them a story each time they go on a car journey. But not every child has this at home. For the children that don't, school has an important role to play: it will be the key factor in a child's reading life.

Think and reflect

Thinking about your own classroom or school:

- Do the children you teach read a wide range of rich texts often?
- How do you encourage children to read often and widely?

(*continued*)

Think and reflect (*continued*)

- Would any of the strategies in Chapter 6 to promote reading work in your context?
- Which ones might have the biggest impact on children's writing?

Chapter 6 suggests some authentic strategies for encouraging children to read widely in their own time, but if we want children to be aware of the ideas and language in books there are additional things we might do to focus their attention while they're engaged in their wider reading:

Oral book reviews – thinking, talking about and sharing language helps us to make sense of the meaning of what we read. While written book reviews and reading journals can be useful to structure children's thinking, they have their problems, not least that we're following up what should be an enjoyable and valuable activity immediately with a forced piece of writing. A better strategy might be giving children time to talk informally about the books they have read and why they have/ haven't enjoyed them. This could be during reading time in school or as a standalone activity. Encouraging children to go beyond the obvious 'I liked this bit . . ./I didn't like that character . . .' and give examples of the language, themes and how the text resonated with their own experiences in terms of both other books and real life can be a powerful way of making them aware of the text.

Golden language – on a similar theme, children can be encouraged to collect *golden language* as they read – words, phrases, sentences or whole poems or paragraphs that they feel are particularly special for some reason. It might be that they are beautiful or that they encapsulate an idea perfectly. It might be that they are funny or unusual. If a child finds an example of what they consider to be *golden language* (and it must be what *they* consider – they can't be wrong about this), then this example is shared with the community. It might be placed on a working wall or displayed in the classroom. Another possibility is to place it on a PowerPoint slide that acts a screensaver to the classroom whiteboard or computer. When the computer goes to sleep, the examples of *golden language* appear: a steady drip of fascinating language for children to see and think about.

Think and reflect

One of the great myths of primary English teaching, especially the teaching of writing, is that some words are somehow inherently 'better' than others. This can lead to multisyllabic or unusual words being shoehorned into writing to 'improve' it or words such as 'said' or 'good' being banned from classrooms. While variety and control of language are crucial, when we are considering a word, either in reading or with an eye to using in it writing, its usefulness in the particular context and its role in communicating meaning should be what drives its selection.

Reading into writing – taught

In addition to the texts that children read independently, there are also the books that are studied in class. Chapter 1 addressed the distinction between these and made a case for ensuring they are as rich and varied as possible. Barrs and Cork (2001) identify three kinds of texts that are particularly useful in supporting children to learn to write:

Traditional tales – these are useful because they offer a clear and regular narrative structure.

Rich and lyrical texts – these contain 'poeticised speech', which enables children to appreciate how figurative language can be used to communicate different effects.

Emotionally powerful texts – these can draw children into a story, causing them to emphasise with characters that they have come to care about. Table 8.1 gives some examples of texts that might fit into each category.

Table 8.1 Texts for stimulating writing

Traditional tales	Poetic texts	Emotionally powerful texts
The Oxford Treasury of Fairy Tales by Geraldine McCaughrean	Moby Dick retold by Geraldine McCaughrean	Emil and the Detectives by Erich Kastner
Myths and Legends retold by Anthony Horowitz	One Thousand and One Arabian Nights by Geraldine McCaughrean	Goodnight Mister Tom by Michelle Magorian
Collected Folk Tales by Alan Garner	Shakespeare Stories by Leon Garfield	Watership Down by Richard Adams
Tales from the West Indies by Faustin Charles	Where my Wellies Take Me by Clare and Michael Morpurgo	El Deafo by Cece Bell
One Thousand and One Arabian Nights by Geraldine McCaughrean	iF- A Treasury of Poems for Almost Every Possibility edited by Allie Esiri and Rachel Kelly	My Name is Mina by David Almond
The Thousand Nights and One Night retold by David Walser		The Miraculous Journey of Edward Tulane by Kate DiCamillo
The Seven Voyages of Sinbad the Sailor retold by John Yeoman	Black Dog by Levi Pinfold	Once by Morris Gleitzman
Grimm Tales by Philip Pullman	Beowulf by Kevin Crossley-Holland	A Bit Lost by Chris Haughton
The Trick of the Tale by John and Caitlin Matthews	The Lie Tree by Frances Hardinge	A Friend for Little Bear by Harry Horse
Aesop's Fables retold by Alice Shirley	Not the End of the World by Geraldine McCaughrean	Charlotte's Web by E. B. White
		The Last Polar Bears by Harry Horse
		A Monster Calls by Patrick Ness
		Grandad's Island by Benji Davies

By studying texts like these, children have the opportunity to draw on them to support their own writing. In the following sections we will consider some ways that rich texts can be used to support writing.

Using texts as a model for writing

Some texts lend themselves to being the model for a specific type of writing. This could be narrative writing, with children reading and enjoying the text before writing a story of their own which will draw on their reading and discussion. While this might involve an element of close study, helping children to see how language choices contribute to a specific effect (more on this in Chapter 9), teaching opportunities need to be broader than simply seeking to imitate a text. Instead, children need opportunities to think about and discuss how features are used for effect and then experiment with them, developing their understanding as they do.

If a text is being read with an eye to eventually being the model for writing, it is tempting to pore over the text and mine it for every possible useful element. This runs the risk of removing all enjoyment from the reading process – death by analysis. In a thoughtful sequence of teaching, children will have the opportunity to think about and enjoy the text, too – to *feel* the effect of the writing, rather than just analyse the effect in a detached way. With a shorter text, such as a picturebook, poem or short story, there might be the chance to read through it first without stopping to talk and pull it apart.

For a longer text such as a novel, the unit could consist of reading or listening to the entire book and stopping at key moments to pull out extracts for closer study. Another approach is *front-loading* the analysis, where the book is studied closely as a model at the beginning of the teaching sequence, then as the children move onto writing their own drafts, the class continue to read the book, but this time for enjoyment and the longer-term benefits of listening to great literature.

Think and reflect

Making use of scaffolds

Writing frames or detailed success criteria can be useful for helping children to create a strong piece of writing, but if over-used, these same practices that help to create a strong piece of writing might actually be a barrier to helping children become accomplished writers. Approaches to teaching writing that rely on a heavily-scaffolded approach or 'a recipe for good writing' (often expressed as a mnemonic) might help to produce individual good pieces of writing, but this could be to the detriment of helping a child to become a good writer in the longer term. Children need to be given the opportunity to write without scaffolds and success criteria if they are to develop the ability to write independently, becoming aware of their audience and purpose and tailoring their writing to these demands. A scaffold can be used to support a piece of writing or introduce a particular idea, but this should always lead to independent writing – there should always be a plan to take the scaffold down.

Using texts instead of text types

Teaching children about different genres of writing (both fiction and non-fiction) can be useful for developing their understanding, as long as these are not taught in an overly prescriptive way. One way to explore different genres of writing, ensuring children think about the purpose and intended audience of each as well as the conventions, is to use texts to model different genres. This works especially well if the texts offer a different perspective, perhaps drawing on elements of more than one text type or subverting the genre. These could be written independently, but the key ways to support children to develop as writers is through use of guided and shared writing (see Chapter 2). Here are some ideas for text to use as a stimulus for writing:

Text: *Instructions* by Neil Gaiman and Charles Vess
Writing task: narrative using instructional language

This exquisite book tells the story of a magical quest as a series of instructions. Writing a similar narrative as a set of direct instructions provides an interesting way for children to practise the language of instructional writing, including the imperative, in a motivating and creative context.

Text: *The Three Little Pigs Advert* by The Guardian newspaper
(*search online to find*)
Writing task: persuasive newspaper article

In school, newspapers are often approached as non-fiction writing, promoting a detached writing style that presents the facts impartially. As adults, we know that this isn't the case and that every newspaper will cover a particular issue differently. Asking children to write two articles, each from a different point of view is a terrific way of practising persuasive writing as well as thinking about bias in the media. A task like this is excellent for challenging very confident writers. For them, the challenge is to communicate their feelings on an issue and persuade the reader in a subtle way. Can they present a biased argument, but make it appear to be balanced? The Guardian newspaper's *Three Little Pigs* advert is a good way of introducing different points of view in reporting.

Text: *DK Find Out! site* by Dorling Kindersley (www.dkfindout. com)
Writing task: online information text

The nature of the texts we interact with has changed greatly in the last few years. While books are often central to what we read and write in schools, online texts are increasingly the most popular way for us to engage with information. An information text that is written to sit online is different to a non-chronological report and therefore it needs different writing skills. Being able to write about a particular topic and then link to another page that gives more detail is an interesting way of exploring how children organise their ideas (and can be useful for explaining the use of paragraphs, for example). Using resources such as *Weebly* to create online texts can be very motivating for children. Sites like *DK Find Out!* give an excellent model to share on the IWB in class.

**Text: *The Many Worlds of Albie Bright* by Christopher Edge
Writing task: combined narrative and non-fiction text**

This wonderful children's book draws on the peculiarities of quantum physics to drive the story. At the same time as sharing a gripping story, the book sheds some light on how the science works through the books that the protagonist reads in the story. Children could choose a scientific idea, perhaps something they're studying in lessons, and use it as the central moment in a story of their own. Or they could reverse this idea. From TED talks to popular science books, using a story as an introduction for explaining an idea is a well-used technique for engaging a reader and making an idea stick. In primary school teaching, it has the added advantage of exploring two different types of writing at the same time, learning about both by considering their different demands. For example, children could tell the story of a famous scientist before they explain a specific concept – for example, Sir Isaac Newton arriving at a theory of gravity or Edward Jenner pioneering vaccination.

In each of these examples children have the opportunity to explore the conventions of a different type of text by using an engaging text as a vehicle to learn about structure and different language features. As children move through the school, the writing that they produce won't fit neatly into one of the Primary Strategy's text types. If we want a generation of children who can use language with confidence, selecting words and phrases to communicate their ideas clearly and powerfully, then we need to teach them be flexible in their writing. Aside from that, playing with the different genres inspired by a text can be a lot of fun, which can be an important end in itself.

Why not try?

While picturebooks are a key feature of a child's reading diet when they are younger, they are less-common higher up the school. This is lost opportunity as many picturebooks written for older readers give a rich, multi-layered reading experience. Books such as *The Island* by Armin Greder or *The Rabbits* by John Marsden and Shaun Tan introduce complicated ideas that lend themselves to deep discussion. The interplay between the pictures and text can provide an additional layer of complexity – a text that appears simple on the surface, such as John Burningham's *Come Away From the Water, Shirley*, will take on another meaning when read alongside the images.

Rich picturebooks are also useful in older year groups in a pragmatic way: like short stories and poems, they provide a way of sharing a whole story or idea in a relatively succinct form. Reading and studying a whole novel can tie up English lessons for many weeks, while a picturebook might introduce the same rich themes in a shorter amount of time.

Some excellent picturebooks for older readers include:

Night of the Gargoyles by Eve Bunting

The Island by Armin Greder

The Tunnel by Anthony Browne

The Arrival by Shaun Tan

Weslandia by Paul Fleischman

FArTHER by Graham Baker-Smith

A more comprehensive list of picturebooks for older readers can be found in Appendix III.

Writing for pleasure

Schools are increasingly aware of the role encouraging children to read in their own time can have on academic achievement (see Chapter 6). The idea of writing for pleasure seems to have a much lower profile. Despite this, time for children to write about what they want can support the development of some key concepts that help children to become keen and confident writers.

Firstly, it helps children to see themselves as writers, rather than as 'people who do some writing when they're told'. This shift in mindset can be incredibly helpful when we're asking them to follow a writing process that involves making changes to their work to improve it. Writing for pleasure also helps children to see writing as a form of communication – the key to good writing isn't necessarily meeting a set of success criteria or adhering to the demands of a specific genre; instead it's about being able to communicate with a reader, to share your ideas lucidly or to use language to persuade, explain or delight. It can also help children to actually enjoy sitting down to write, and as with everything else, teaching writing is easier to teach if we're working with willing participants. Finally, children's own writing gives us a medium through which to teach the craft of writing. On a simple level, if children have got a piece of writing in front of them that they're interested in and are already pleased with, they are more likely to be motivated to work to improve it because of the investment they have in the piece of writing is likely to be greater. And it's through making these changes that children learn to write well for a particular audience and purpose. Writing for pleasure doesn't need to replace the normal business of teaching writing, but nor should it be seen in opposition to it either. Hopefully, school-initiated writing would be both pleasurable and educationally valuable. In addition to time spent writing for pleasure, the normal business of teaching children to write needs to continue: children need English lessons full of shared and guided writing; the chance to look at texts and identify how great authors and storytellers use language for effect; the chance to write, receive feedback and then edit or redraft in the light of that feedback; and focused grammar and punctuation teaching. Most children won't grow as writers by simply writing lots: they will need to be taught how to control language for effect too.

Think and reflect

In practical terms writing for pleasure might work best where the teacher:

Doesn't dictate the content – this can be tricky as children's free writing is likely to be filled with children's television characters and name-checks for children's friends in the class. It is important to remember that the purpose with this writing isn't to produce work that is interesting for adults (although hopefully it will contribute to that in the longer term); it is about creating an enthusiasm for writing which can be applied to a child's wider writing. It is also about children seeing themselves as a writer with their own unique voice.

Thinks carefully about setting writing as homework – while encouraging free writing at home can be useful as it helps children to practise their writing, freeing up time in school, it is important to think about equity. Some children will have the inclination to write at home, some won't. Some will have support from parents, others won't. Some children will lack the resources (even a paper and pencil) or a quiet space to sit and write. If writing can't or won't happen at home, space for it to happen needs to be found in school so as not to disadvantage anyone.

Share a prompt – often the opportunity for children to write about anything they like for pure pleasure will be met with at least one 'I don't know what to write'. Giving children an optional prompt – a picture, a film clip, an artefact, a title or an idea is absolutely fine. Better still is a choice of starting points with the freedom to deviate from it if a good idea comes along.

Don't call it 'writing for pleasure' – this suggests that all other writing isn't done for pleasure, but is a chore that must be tolerated. 'Free-choice writing', 'personal writing' or 'golden writing' are all alternatives that avoid setting the writing that is done of children's own free will in opposition to the writing they are required to do at school.

This chapter has looked at texts as the starting point for writing in the widest sense. Another key aspect of writing is the transcription element – grammar, punctuation and spelling. In the next chapter we'll consider how rich and engaging texts can support children's use of grammar and punctuation.

In summary

- Although we are not sure exactly how reading influences writing, research and experience tell us that these two facets of English are linked
- The quantity, quality and range of children's reading can all have an impact on the language and ideas they can draw on when they write
- Texts can be used as a direct model for writing or as a broad stimulus
- Texts can be an effective way of demonstrating and inspiring forms of writing that do not fit neatly into a specific genre
- Writing that is done for pure pleasure, separate from the demands of curriculum writing, can be motivating and can play an important role in supporting children's development in writing

Bibliography

Barrs, M. and Cork, V. (2001) *The Reader in the Writer*. London: Centre for Language in Primary Education.

Dockrell, J. E. and Connelly, V. (2009) The impact of oral language skills on the production of written text. In V. Connelly, A. L. Barnett, J. E. Dockrell, and A. Tolmie (eds) *Teaching and Learning Writing* (pp. 45–62). Leicester: British Psychological Society.

King, S. (2012) *On Writing: A Memoir of the Craft*. London: Hodder and Stoughton.

Literature and multi-media texts

Come Away from the Water, Shirley by John Burningham
DK Find Out! site by Dorling Kindersley
Instructions by Neil Gaiman and Charles Vess
The Island by Armin Greder
The Many Worlds of Albie Bright by Christopher Edge
The Rabbits by John Marsden and Shaun Tan
The Three Little Pigs Advert by The Guardian newspaper

Teaching grammar and punctuation

Using language features for effect

Words, phrases and clauses are not simply neutral grammatical structures which are naturally acquired; they are the essential semiotic resource for meaning-making in print or on screen. The choice of a verb, the shape of a sentence, the connotation of a metaphor each subtly shift and nuance the potential meaning in a text in the same way that paralinguistic features such as body language, intonation and emphasis do in speech.

(Myhill and Fisher, 2010)

If writing is about communication, then control of language features such as vocabulary and grammar are what allows a writer to communicate with precision and elegance.

The 2014 National Curriculum (DfE, 2013) places significant emphasis on children using grammar and punctuation accurately in their writing. This, combined with the introduction of a national test of grammar, punctuation and spelling at the end of Key Stage 2 in England, has led to a focus being placed on teaching the technical aspects of English. The curriculum specifies what should be taught to each year group in detail, providing teachers with a shared terminology for different aspects (*inverted commas* rather than *speech marks* or *single-clause sentences* instead of *simple sentences,* for example). What the curriculum doesn't do is provide teachers with *how* to teach these language features, stating that all of this content provides merely 'the structure on which to construct exciting lessons' (DfE, 2013).

Attitudes to teaching grammar and punctuation can be seen as sitting somewhere along a spectrum that stretches from advocating purely *discrete grammar teaching* (children learning about an aspect of grammar from a teacher or textbook and learning the rules of how it works, without a link to a text) to *fully embedded grammar teaching* (where any grammar or punctuation are taught as they naturally occur in the books children read). In reality, the English-language teaching that happens in most classrooms is a mixture of these two approaches, although perhaps favouring one approach or the other.

Research suggests that grammar teaching that is completely decontextualised from the teaching of reading and writing has little impact on the quality of children's writing (Jones *et al.*, 2013). In contrast, explicit teaching of English-language features that makes use of 'discussion, exploration, investigation and experimentation' can support children to tailor specific aspects of language for certain effects (Myhill *et al.*, 2012). This *contextualised grammar teaching* draws on both discrete and embedded approaches: teaching grammar in the context of real writing (from published texts, everyday language use and children's writing), but 'is explicit about how language works, and about how language choices construct meanings in different contexts, using the correct grammatical terminology as part of that explicitness' (Myhill *et al.*, 2016). This view of grammar teaching is reflected in the 2014 National Curriculum, which states that 'building this knowledge [of grammar] is best achieved through a focus on grammar within the teaching of reading, writing and speaking' (DfE, 2013).

Starting with great texts

One of the most effective ways to teach help children to be aware of and to control different language features is to start with a rich text. Learning about language through the context of high quality writing, rather than through a series of exercises on grammar and punctuation, enables children to see how language really works. It can help them to understand how and why writers have made specific choices with language and they can also learn about the relationship between grammar and punctuation, that is, that they do not work independently of one another. In this chapter we will look at three ways that a text-based curriculum can support children's knowledge and application of grammar and punctuation:

- Developing a 'feel for language'
- Sharing examples of language features (and terminology) being used for effect
- Providing a direct model for children's own writing

Developing a 'feel for language'

The stop–start nature of spoken English means that the words we speak in conversation are hardly ever organised into grammatically-complete sentences and, apart from in very formal situations, the language we use tends to be different to written English. This means that books are often the most important source of new language once children are of school age (Elley, 1989). This is true of children's growing vocabularies, but it's also true of different grammatical constructions and sentence structures. The more children read, the more likely they are to come across new words and new ways of organising them into the sort of sentences that are useful for communicating in writing.

If children don't choose to read in their own time, then making time in school for them to read a wide range of good quality texts is an obvious way of supporting their language development.

Creating time to read aloud to children and for children to read independently right the way through the school are effective strategies for developing a feeling for language. Listening to texts than children might not be able to read alone allows children to absorb new language without being limited to the texts they can read independently. This is especially important for younger children, whose word-reading skills will probably lag behind their language comprehension. For older children it provides access to texts that they might not choose to read themselves and it is especially valuable for children who lack the reading stamina or inclination to read challenging texts independently. It also gives the teacher the opportunity to stop and discuss the meaning of words, phrases or specific constructions (and why they've been chosen by an author) as they read, supporting children's understanding as they go.

Working within a curriculum where there is a body of grammar and punctuation knowledge to teach, sustained independent reading and listening to a book being read aloud might sound like woolly or indulgent activities, but they can have significant impact on children's language development.

Sharing examples of language features (and terminology) being used for effect

A successful model for contextualised grammar teaching will balance discrete grammar teaching that shows children *how* a particular language feature works with embedded grammar teaching that shows *why* an author might have chosen a particular grammatical construction in order to create a particular effect. Firstly, the particular grammatical or punctuation feature is shared with children from a real context – a book, newspaper or a website, perhaps. This way the children can see the language feature being used by an expert, enabling children to think about how and why writers have made specific choices with the language they use. Take the colon in the sentence below:

> *The new exercise regime was showing results: Tom was almost ready for the race.*

The children can pause to discuss what the colon is communicating here, that the second clause in the sentence *follows on* from the first. The training Tom is doing *has caused* him to become fitter ready for his race.

Then children can learn about the specific language feature and the rules for using it. This might involve discussion about the other uses of a colon (introducing items in a list, say) and the children could undertake some practice activities to embed their knowledge. But this phase doesn't need to be prescriptive. In this case, the children could consider some of the alternatives to using a colon, discussing how these might subtly affect the meaning.

The new exercise regime was showing results and Tom was almost ready for the race.
The new exercise regime was showing results; Tom was almost ready for the race.
The new exercise regime was showing results. Tom was almost ready for the race.

Discussion can then focus on why the author has chosen to use a colon over the other acceptable alternatives and whether they think he made the right choice.

Combining more than one language feature

The real benefits of using a high-quality text as a starting point for teaching grammar and punctuation can be seen when children are given the opportunity to explore how different language structures can be combined to create effective writing. For example, considering the first description of Elmer the Elephant in David McKee's *Elmer*, where Elmer is described with a list of nine colours joined together with the conjunction 'and'. The teacher might then discuss how the very long sentence listing Elmer's colours breaks 'the rules' about how many clauses a sentence should have and how many times you can use the word 'and', but that it does this very deliberately for effect. Children will find reading the sentence aloud in one breath a real struggle – the jumble of words cascading out of their mouths emphasising just how many colours his patchwork is made up of.

A Key Stage 2 example might be the opening to chapter 3 of Kenneth Grahame's *The Wind in the Willows*. This section provides a rich example of how grammar, punctuation and sentence structure work together to create atmosphere. The teacher could work sentence-by-sentence through the scene where Mole finds himself alone in the Wild Wood, identifying and discussing how the language the author chooses shows Mole's terror at what he finds there: longer, multi-clause sentences convey Mole's growing confusion:

He ran up against things, he fell over and into things, he darted under things and dodged around things.

The scene features repeated one-sentence paragraphs to show the level of danger building, moment-by-moment:

Then the faces began.
Then the whistling began.
Then the pattering began.

Repetition of words within sentences shows Mole's hesitancy:

And he – he was alone.

Throughout the chapter the author uses questions to put the reader into the role of Mole:

Was it in front or behind?
Hunting, chasing, closing in round something – or somebody?
Perhaps even safety, but who could tell?

The whole scene is a masterclass in writing for suspense and examples like these are important to study as they illustrate how more than one language feature can work with others to create an effect.

Think and reflect

While analysing a text to see how language is used to create a specific effect is an important part of learning about grammar and punctuation, care should be taken to ensure that this doesn't dominate English teaching. If every time the children read a text they must then analyse it, this can detract from their enjoyment of the text and their wider appreciation of what they are reading. While it is tempting to make a teaching point from the texts that we share with children, it should be used sparingly to avoid 'death by analysis'.

Providing a direct model for children's own writing

As we saw in Chapter 7, there are many elements for to children juggle when they write. When composing, beginner writers often find themselves focusing on *what* to write, rather than to *how* they make use of different language constructions to express themselves.

While continued exposure to great writing will give them a model for writing in a broad sense, occasionally using a text as a direct model can be useful for showing children how different language structures work.

One way of doing this is using a short extract from a text as a template for children's own writing – a technique called *overwriting*. *Overwriting* is where children follow an author's writing word-by-word replacing the text with their own ideas. This works particularly well in shared writing sessions (see page 29), with the original on the IWB being discussed and then overwritten as a class. By matching their writing to that of the author's, the group can discuss the language choices that have been made.

Obviously, an approach like *overwriting* that uses direct imitation should be used sparingly and for a particular teaching purpose. Like any scaffold for supporting children to be able to do something, there needs to be a plan to remove it once it has served its purpose, moving the children towards being able to use the technique they've explored independently. As Myhill *et al.* note: 'Imitation is not the same as copying – it involves some kind of re-creation of grammatical patterns or ideas, rather than a direct duplication, and is best thought of as a scaffold that allows children to try out new structures and play with new forms of expression' (Myhill *et al.*, 2016).

Approaches like this are common when children are younger (with children following the structure of Eric Carle's *The Very Hungry Caterpillar* to write their own stories, for example), but they are less-common in Key Stage 2. To be most effective, a direct imitation technique like *overwriting* will work through a set of clear steps:

1. **Choose an interesting piece of text**
    The text the children are going to imitate needs to show an interesting example of language being used for a particular effect. The teacher

needs to make clear the link between the grammatical construction and the intended audience and purpose. For example, a rich non-fiction text is rarely written as a simple list of facts. Instead we have something carefully constructed to sound interesting and authoritative:

The Atacama Desert is the driest desert on Earth and yet, perhaps surprisingly, it is rich with life. Although it receives only a little rainfall each year, this 1000-mile strip of land wedged between the Andes Mountains and Pacific Ocean in South America is home to many creatures, including penguins.

2. **Read it together and analyse its structure**
   This is a key step in helping children to become better writers. As teachers, we need to make them aware that the words in the text haven't appeared by magic; instead they've been carefully chosen by a writer to create a specific effect. It is this control of language that children need to develop in order to become confident writers. In the extract above, the teacher might draw children's attention to the use of the phrase 'and yet' functioning as a conjunction to set up a contradiction between the two clauses. This is supported by the embedded phrase 'perhaps surprisingly'. The second sentence builds on the first, using a subordinate clause to give the reader some information about the rainfall, followed by the main clause giving additional information about the desert and its inhabitants. The overall effect is an informative and mature piece of writing that is far more engaging than a series of short sentences about the desert:

The Atacama Desert is the driest desert on Earth. It is rich with life. It receives only a little rainfall each year. It is a 1000-mile strip of land wedged between the Andes Mountains and Pacific Ocean in South America. It is home to many creatures, including penguins.

3. **Overwrite with different content**
   The next step is to work as a group or whole class to overwrite this as a piece of shared writing. This gives the teacher the opportunity to model the writing process and helps the children to think about

the structure of the text. The core structure of the text is kept, but the topic is changed from a desert to a coral reef:

The Atacama Desert is the driest desert on Earth and yet, perhaps surprisingly, it is rich with life. Although it receives only a little rainfall each year, this 1000-mile strip of land wedged between the Andes Mountains and Pacific Ocean in South America is home to many creatures, including penguins.

The Great Barrier Reef is the largest coral reef on Earth and yet, perhaps surprisingly, it is made of billions of tiny living creatures called polyps. Although it is home to many creatures including 1500 species of fish and six types of turtle, this protected nature reserve is under threat from pollution and climate change.

If children were simply asked to write about the Great Barrier Reef, it is unlikely that many would have structured their writing like this.

4. Independent writing (with some reminders)

The next step is for children to use some of the structures they've learnt in their independent writing. As well as giving lots of time to practise, it can be helpful to remind children about what they've learnt in previous sessions before they write: 'it would be great to see you using some of the sentence structures we used when we were writing about the Great Barrier Reef'. Some children almost need permission to use the techniques they've been practising in their own work. It is likely that some children will need teacher or peer support to do this. Some children will also make mistakes and will need some feedback to improve their writing. As we've seen in Chapter 7, giving children the chance to learn from their mistakes and make corrections and improvements are both key features of good writing teaching.

While an imitation approach to teaching writing can seem very restrictive and counter to the idea of children expressing their own writing voice, it's worth remembering that this is just one tool in a teacher's armoury for teaching writing. It is one approach amongst many that can be used sparingly to help children to develop awareness of the choices authors make about language and the effect these decisions have on a reader.

Think and reflect

Think about the teaching of grammar and punctuation in your own school or classroom. Are there opportunities for children to:

- Listen to and reflect on the way language is used in rich texts?
- Learn how the different grammar and punctuation features they have seen work discretely?
- Use the models of language they have learnt about in their own writing?

This 'sandwich model' of grammar teaching – seeing a language feature used for effect, learning how it works and then using it in their own extended writing – can be a powerful way of helping children to use grammar and punctuation for effect.

Using rich texts to drive the teaching of grammar and punctuation, whether as a very focused model or more widely, gives children the opportunity to understand a specific aspect of grammar or punctuation and learn the terminology and 'rules' about its use that are vital for using it accurately in their own writing. More importantly, they have the opportunity to see a particular language feature being used for effect by a skilled writer; something that a decontextualised grammar activity won't provide.

The next chapter will consider spoken language and the relationship between this and the other elements of English.

In summary

- Decontextualised teaching of grammar – working through a set of textbook exercises – is useful for passing a grammar test, but has limited impact on the quality of children's writing

(*continued*)

In summary (*continued*)

- As important as learning different rules for language use is developing a feel for language – being able to identify what sounds right and what doesn't

- Reading and discussing great writing shows children how grammar and punctuation can be used to create a particular effect

- Texts can be used as a direct model or be absorbed as models for language over the longer term

- A sandwich model of grammar teaching brings together the most useful features of explicit and embedded grammar teaching, enabling children to see how a specific language feature works, learn the rules behind it and then use it in their own writing

Bibliography

DfE (2013) *National Curriculum in England: Primary Curriculum*. London: DfE.

Elley, W. B. (1989) Vocabulary acquisition from listening to stories. *Reading Research Quarterly*, 24 (2), 174–187.

Jones, S. M., Myhill, D. A. and Bailey, T. C. (2013) Grammar for writing? An investigation into the effect of contextualised grammar teaching on student writing. *Reading and Writing*, 26 (8), 1241–1263.

Myhill, D. and Fisher, R. (2010) Editorial: Writing development: cognitive, sociocultural, linguistic perspectives. *Journal of Research in Reading*, 33 (1), 1–3.

Myhill, D., Jones, S., Lines, H. and Watson, A. (2012) Re-thinking grammar: the impact of embedded grammar teaching on children's writing and children's metalinguistic understanding. *Research Papers in Education*, 21 (2), 139–166.

Myhill, D., Jones, S., Watson, A. and Lines, H. (2016) *Essential Primary Grammar*. Maidenhead: Open University Press.

Children's books

Elmer by David McKee
The Very Hungry Caterpillar by Eric Carle
The Wind in the Willows by Kenneth Grahame

PART 4
Teaching English by the book

Spoken language

The importance of oracy

Spoken language sits at the heart of English teaching, reflected in James Britton's often-quoted words that 'reading and writing float on a sea of talk' (Britton, 1970). But spoken language is not simply a precursor to reading and writing; it is through the language we hear and use that we make sense of the world:

> Children, we now know, need to talk and to experience a rich diet of spoken language, in order to think and to learn. Reading, writing and number may be the acknowledged curriculum 'basics', but talk is arguably the true foundation of learning.
>
> Alexander (2004)

The development of spoken language is an important area of the curriculum in its own right, but it is also the medium through which learning happens. As it is intrinsically linked to the development of reading and writing, previous chapters have also considered aspects of spoken language. While the development of spoken language weaves through the chapters of the book, this chapter specifically considers how rich texts can provide children with opportunities to develop their spoken language, focusing on:

- Giving an opportunity for discussion and dialogue
- Providing a stimulus for debate
- Texts as a model for classroom language

Discussion and dialogue

Alexander (2001) organises classroom talk into five categories:

- **Rote** – drilling of facts, ideas and routines
- **Recitation** – questions designed to elicit recall or work out answers from clues in the question
- **Instruction or exposition** – giving information and explaining facts, principles and procedures
- **Discussion** – the exchange of ideas with a view to sharing information and solving problems
- **Dialogue** – achieving common understanding through structured, cumulative questioning and discussion which guide and prompt, reduce choices, minimise risk and error and expedite 'handover' of concepts and principles

While all of these types of talk are needed for specific purposes in the classroom, it is discussion and dialogue that are most useful for helping children to think and reason. And a rich text can be a useful starting point for these interactions. Genuine dialogue to develop children's understanding, whether as a whole class, in pairs or between the teacher and child, depends on authenticity: asking questions that require a genuine answer rather than one the teacher is expecting (Nystrand, 2006). For genuine discussion to flourish, the classroom climate needs to be one where children feel free to share their ideas and expose their misconceptions without fear of giving the wrong answer or revealing that they have misunderstood. This is another benefit of authentic classroom talk: there will be many correct responses.

This type of talk, where children have the opportunity to share their knowledge and opinions, agree and disagree and defend their views politely and constructively, is the ideal for book talk. Roche (2014) argues that while reading and listening to books are important activities, these regular opportunities for thinking, interaction and rich book talk are necessary if children are to develop strong oral language skills and vocabulary.

However, this type of talk doesn't come naturally to most children and it is only through practice (and modelling from peers and adults) that they are able to interact in this way. While some may get this from home, for many children school will be where they develop this ability. This model for classroom talk has been discussed throughout the book, with advice on effective questioning in Chapter 4, how dialogue can be built into the curriculum in Chapter 3 and examples of questions and discussion points in the units of work in Appendix II.

Debate

A text-based curriculum for English provides more than just developing children's literacy skills. Studying and discussing rich works of literature can introduce children to new ideas and concepts.

Many great texts introduce children to characters and situations that are open to interpretation, with subtle shades of meaning that don't lend themselves to forming easy opinions. Debating the issues arising from a text is a valuable classroom activity, both for the development of children's' understanding of texts, their spoken language and the ways it can link to wider learning experiences, such as understanding issues and empathising with characters and their situations. This may happen in an informal way through classroom discussion or through a more formal debating structure. Debating an issue from an informed opinion requires some knowledge and understanding of the subject if the debate is to move beyond very simple arguments. Having read a book or become familiar with the world of a story, children have the necessary knowledge to construct their arguments, linking these with their own ideas and knowledge from outside of the text. If the book or story is one the children have developed an emotional attachment to, then they may be motivated to argue their case more convincingly too.

A challenging task can be to give children the job of defending a particular position, especially one that might seem indefensible, such as defending a villain in a court trial. In many rich books there will be a logic to the antagonist's actions and a reason for them behaving like they do. Even if the children don't agree with the actions, an activity like this can support understanding or build empathy.

The story of *Macbeth* is a perfect story for debate. Planning the debate around statements such as:

Macbeth is ultimately responsible for King Duncan's Death

can prompt discussion between children given different sides of the argument. While one side may argue that Macbeth is responsible as it is he who commits the physical act of murder, another group may be tasked with arguing that responsibility lies with Lady Macbeth who urged her husband or the Weird Sisters who prophesised the murder.

A text like *Would You Rather ...* by John Burningham, while covering very different subject matter, can also be a useful tool for debate. Each page provides motivating subject matter: would it be better to eat slug dumplings or drink snail squash; to make magic with a fairy or be naughty with an imp? Again, while these texts appear very different, both can provide the catalyst for a class debate following a similar structure:

1. Initial vote – before they have been told which side of the argument they will be representing, the children to vote to decide if they agree with the statement or not. Votes are counted and recorded.

2. Organise the groups – the children are placed into teams for each side of the argument. That might mean two teams in the case of the Macbeth statement or more if the text provides that choice. For *Would You Rather ...* , children could be placed into teams to argue that it is best to be:

   - lost in the fog
   - lost at sea
   - lost in a desert
   - lost in a forest
   - lost in a crowd

3. Prepare arguments – each group needs time to prepare their arguments, focusing on positives of their argument (why their side of the argument is right) and the weaknesses of the other side (why the other side is wrong).

4. Present – each group has a short period of time to make their case as persuasively as they can.

5. Questions – after the children have listened to each other's presentations, allow time for the groups to ask each other questions and respond.

6. Final vote – ask the children to vote again. Have their choices changed? Have any groups been successful in persuading their classmates to change their mind?

Texts as a model for classroom language

Both the 2014 National Curriculum and the Teacher Standards for England require teachers to promote children's use of 'Standard English' in the classroom. In this context, Standard English:

> . . . can be recognised by the use of a very small range of forms such as *those books, I did it* and *I wasn't doing anything* (rather than their non-Standard equivalents); it is not limited to any particular accent. It is the variety of English which is used, with only minor variation, as a major world language. Some people use Standard English all the time, in all situations from the most casual to the most formal, so it covers most registers.
>
> (DfE, 2013)

It is what Crystal (1995) calls 'a minority variety (identified chiefly by its vocabulary, grammar and orthography) which carries most prestige and is most widely understood'. Standard English is the variety of English most closely associated with powerful institutions and is useful in formal situations. While it is the native spoken dialect of only around 15% of the country, it is also the variety of English that most closely matches written English. Being able to move from a local dialect to Standard English and back again is incredibly useful for children's writing (Bex and Watts, 1999).

While the two are often conflated, Standard English isn't the same as formal language. Informal Standard English uses contractions (wouldn't, isn't), colloquial language (*mates*, *the Rec*) and abbreviations (*TV* instead of *television*), but does not use features of non-Standard English such as double negatives (*he hasn't got none*) and dialect-specific subject-verb agreement (*we was* instead of *we were*). Thinking about the two things and sorting phrases and sentences into formal and informal, Standard and non-Standard can be a useful way of making this distinction.

Think and reflect

Standard English and accent

Children sometimes need to be reminded that it is perfectly possible to use Standard English constructions in any accent at all. Sometimes accent gets mixed up with the structure of language, especially if children are encouraged to switch to Standard English by 'using a posh voice' or 'speaking like the Queen'. These two ways of introducing Standard English should be avoided at all costs as they make Standard English something 'other': a way of speaking used by people 'who aren't like us'.

Listening to the same sentence or line of dialogue from a book read aloud in different accents can be useful in helping children to see that the words stay the same, even if the *way* they are pronounced is different.

Myhill *et al.* (2016) suggest five principles for approaching the teaching of Standard English:

- Focus on understanding language and knowledge about language, rather than 'correctness'

- Talk about both Standard and non-Standard English
- Encourage language investigation, especially of local dialects
- Remember that language variation is not just regional, but social too
- Support children in becoming confident code-switchers – able to use SE with ease where appropriate

Much of the spoken language use, apart from in very formal situations such as presentations, doesn't follow the same patterns of language as Standard English. Sentences often trail off unfinished, non-verbal clues such as gestures are used to supplement missing words and the variety of sentence structures can be limited. It is through reading written text that children are able to encounter and ultimately absorb the vocabulary and syntax of formal written English, developing control over increasingly sophisticated language patterns that exist in written language, such as noun phrases for clarity of meaning, phrasal verbs and different types of subordination (Perera, 1984; Allison *et al.*, 2002).

Why not try?

Texts that contrast characters speaking in ways other than Standard English are useful for helping children to think about what is a standard construction and what is not. These include texts where characters speak in regional dialects, archaic language or other non-standard speech patterns. Some useful texts for this are:

One Thousand and One Arabian Nights by Geraldine McCaughrean

I Yam a Donkey by Cece Bell

The BFG by Roald Dahl

Shakespeare Stories by Leon Garfield

The Raven by Edgar Allen Poe

The Red Badge of Courage by Stephen Crane

(continued)

Why not try? (*continued*)

Gawain and the Green Knight retold by Philip Reeve

Just So Stories by Rudyard Kipling

How the Whale Became by Ted Hughes

The Owl Service by Alan Garner

Dis Poetry by Benjamin Zephaniah

Listen Mr Oxford Don by John Agard

While it can be thought of as a discrete area of the curriculum to be taught, spoken language runs like a thread through all aspects of classroom life. Through the approaches to teaching English and the curriculum design outlined in this book, there are three ideas that will help children's spoken language to develop by making use of a rich text-based curriculum:

- Rich texts give children a model for language that isn't often represented in speech. Time to read and talk about books gives children access to this formal language. This helps them to recognise different types of language, enabling them to code-switch to the variety of spoken English that supports their writing and allows their voice to be taken seriously

- Reading widely on its own isn't enough. It is through rich dialogue and discussion around books that children have the opportunity to stretch their thinking, form opinions and then defend these opinions. It is through high-quality talk that children explore new ideas and, ultimately, learn new things

- The characters and situations presented in rich texts are often ambiguous and open to interpretation, requiring thought and empathy on the part of the reader. This provides the opportunity for children to think about and then discuss or debate these ideas. This potential for high-level discussion is why a text-based curriculum can be so valuable beyond simply helping children to become better readers and writers

In summary

- Spoken language development is important as the foundation to reading and writing, but it is also an important end in itself; it is the medium through which we think and learn

- Of the different forms of classroom language modes, discussion and dialogue are the most valuable for children's learning in English; opportunities for these need to be planned carefully

- Rich texts provide opportunities for children to debate, helping them to consider issues and ideas outside of their immediate sphere of experience

- Written texts provide a model for the different, more-formal language structures that are useful for a range of different contexts, including much of the writing that is required to communicate successfully at school

Bibliography

Alexander, R. J. (2001) *Culture and Pedagogy: International Comparisons in Primary Education.* Oxford: Blackwell.

Alexander, R. J. (2004) *Towards Dialogic Teaching: Rethinking Classroom Talk.* Cambridge: Dialogos.

Allison, P., Beard, R., and Willcocks, J. (2002) Subordination in children's writing. *Language and Education: An International Journal,* 16 (2), 97–111.

Bex, T. and Watts, R. J. (eds) (1999) *Standard English: The Widening Debate.* London: Routledge.

Britton, J. (1970) *Language and Learning.* Coral Gables, FL: University of Miami Press.

Crystal, D. (1995) *The Cambridge Encyclopaedia of the English Language,* 2nd ed. Cambridge: Cambridge University Press.

DfE (2013) *National Curriculum in England: Primary Curriculum.* London: DfE.

Myhill, D., Jones, S., Watson, A. and Lines, H. (2016) *Essential Primary Grammar.* Maidenhead: Open University Press.

Nystrand, M. (2006) Research on the role of classroom discourse as it affects reading comprehension. *Research into the Teaching of Reading*, 40 (4), 392–412.

Perera, K. (1984) *Children's Writing and Reading: Analysing Classroom Language.* Oxford: Blackwell.

Roche, M. (2014) *Developing Children's Critical Thinking through Picture-books.* London: Routledge.

Literature

Macbeth by William Shakespeare
Would You Rather . . . by John Burningham

Drama

Bringing texts to life

As well as being an important art form in its own right, drama can play an invaluable role in supporting a rich text-based English curriculum. The types of drama that children experience in primary school range from play and free-improvisation in the home corner or role-play area, to a scripted nativity or class assembly performance. Drama in all its forms can support understanding in reading, provide a model for writing and develop children's spoken language. But the best primary drama also allows children to work creatively and collaboratively.

Drama in the primary classroom tends to take one of three forms:

- Drama as performance
- Play-based drama
- The use of drama conventions in English lessons

Each of these aspects of drama is important and has a part to play in a text-based curriculum.

Drama as performance

In a text-based curriculum, children should have the opportunity to read play-scripts and perform them to an audience. While it is possible to study a play without ever reading it aloud or performing it, it is not until it is brought to life that the meaning of the words can be fully understood. As well as the inherent value in performing in front of an audience, this form of drama gives children the opportunity to explore the purpose of the writing. The benefits of performance extend beyond understanding and appreciation of a text, as putting on a performance, even in a small group in class, requires concentration, negotiation and teamwork. Over the course of a primary curriculum, performances might include performing existing scripts, writing scripts based on texts written as prose and devising and performing improvised pieces based on a story. Winston and Tandy (1998) suggest that an ensemble approach to devising and performing is especially useful as it promotes a model where:

> . . . groups discuss and work through ideas together, creating theatre as a living text with scripts tending to emerge from, rather than predetermine, the making of the drama. Such a model for devising texts is very adaptable to time, space, the numbers involved in the production and the particular talents of individuals, whereas most playtexts will tend to set these requirements in advance, regardless, of course, of particular contextual considerations. Within performance, such a model removes the star category, once again emphasising group work and partnership, placing complementary demands upon the performers rather than offering great challenges to the few and very little to challenge the many.
>
> (Winston and Tandy, 1998)

As with performing poetry aloud, performing a script or improvised drama to an audience allows children to speak aloud, developing both confidence and refining public speaking techniques.

Play-based drama

In contrast to performance-led drama, improvised play-based drama is still concerned with acting, but it is acting *as* a character, rather than performing a given role written by someone else. Of the types of drama, perhaps this is the one that offers the greatest potential for being used in a text-based approach. Playing sits at the heart of how young children explore new ideas and build their understanding of the world. As children grow older, opportunities for a play-based approach to learning can be limited. Playful drama that gives children the opportunity to explore stories, characters and issues can have a significant impact on children's learning, both in a traditional sense, as recognised by an impact on their understanding, and through writing, but also in other aspects of education such as confidence, thinking and reasoning, imaginative development and the possibility to consider multiple perspectives. While this type of drama is common in the early years of primary school through tasks set using the role-play area (The Three Bears' cottage or the lighthouse from *The Lighthouse Keeper's Lunch*) or with the teacher in role or making use of a puppet – this approach can also be used in Key Stage 2 to great effect, as illustrated by this short cross-curricular unit of work on the poem *Flannan Isle* by Wilfrid Wilson Gibson:

Year 4 text-based unit: *Flannan Isle* by Wilfrid Wilson Gibson

The poem tells the true story of Flannan Isle lighthouse, which stands on an island in the Outer Hebrides off the coast of Scotland. In 1900 the lighthouse was found abandoned by the crew of the relief ship *Hesperus*, the three crewmen having mysteriously disappeared. The poem can be found by searching online. A teaching sequence drawing on play-based drama could be structured as:

1. **Children and teacher in role**
   The lesson begins with children imagining they are the crew of the *Hesperus* – a ship sailing to relieve the crew of the Flannan Isle lighthouse. The teacher (in role as the head of the lighthouse service) tells the children that nothing has been heard from the three men who man the lighthouse for two weeks. The children are to investigate the mystery and find the men. At the moment the class don't know that the story is taken from a poem or that it is a real event.

2. **Improvised drama activity**
   In role, the children investigate a 'crime scene' (set up by the teacher earlier – a table and three chairs, some plates – the children's imagination will fill in the rest). The teacher tells the story of the crew's

journey to the island in a small boat and the walk across the barren ground to the lighthouse's sun-scorched door. The poem describes a table laid for a meal with the food untouched. The door to the room has been left ajar and one of the chairs has been knocked over. Aside from this, there is no sign of the lighthouse men anywhere on the island. The children have time to explore the scene and talk as a group about what may have happened to the men.

3. **Speculation and debate**

   Back in the classroom, the children can begin to develop some theories about the mystery and debate them as a whole class, with the children challenged to justify their opinion of what may have happened.

4. **Read and discuss the poem**

   Next, the children can be given a copy of the poem to read in pairs. Hopefully there will be flickers of recognition and comments from children as the poem goes on and they begin to recognise the story.

5. **Discuss the poem**

   Then the group can read though the poem together, discussing any unfamiliar language and ensuring everyone understands what is happening. Once they have read and discussed it together, the teacher can draw out specific areas of learning, depending on the focus for the group and the session. These might include:

   - *Comprehension* – can the children follow the story? Do they understand the language used?
   - *Word-reading* – can the class read and deduce the meaning of any unfamiliar words?
   - *Structure of poems* – can the class recognise the rhyming pattern or the number of stanzas?
   - *Grammar, punctuation and spelling* – can the children identify the purpose behind different language features (for example, use of semi-colons or apostrophes to denote contractions)?
   - *Writer's craft* – how does Wilfrid Wilson Gibson communicate the feelings of the crew exploring the island? Does he offer any further clues to the men's fate?

6. **Research the real story**

The next stage is to reveal to the children that not only is the story they acted out in drama a famous poem, but it is also a historical event. This is generally greeted with excitement and some disbelief. The children can then research the disappearance itself, perhaps producing presentations or written reports of their findings.

7. **Improvise the story**

The children can work in small groups to create a short drama performance of the lighthouse crew's disappearance. These can be shared with the rest of the class, who can offer feedback.

Play-based improvised drama can provide a motivating way of exploring a text and moving between the world of the drama and the text itself, but its use should always be flexible, reflecting the teacher's preferred way of working and the intended outcomes for children's learning.

The use of drama conventions in English lessons

While drama can play a central role in exploring a text, either through performance or an improvised play-based approach, specific dramatic conventions can also be useful in the context of day-to-day English teaching. Many techniques that have been taken from drama are common features of primary English lessons and can be used to engage children with a text, to further develop their understanding or as a starting-point for writing. Useful drama conventions include:

Character on the wall – the outline of a character from a story is drawn and the children can annotate this with information, predictions and opinions. This might be a way of devising a character or collecting thoughts about a character already known to the group.

Text-based example: *Macbeth* from *Shakespeare Stories* by Leon Garfield

An outline of Lady Macbeth could be placed on the wall or floor and information, opinions and quotes could be added as the story unfolds. Children could then use these notes when writing character studies of

Lady Macbeth or when writing scenes intended to show her thoughts and feelings through her actions.

Hot-seating – a character from the drama is interviewed by the group about his or her behaviour or thoughts. As well as the teacher, different members of the class can take the role of the same character.

Text-based example: *A Friend for Little Bear* by Harry Horse

After listening to the story and acting it out, the children can take it in turns to be hot-seated as Little Bear to answer questions and explain how they are feeling at different points in the story. The pictures from the text could be used to prompt the children to consider Little Bear in different scenes. This could be a worthwhile exercise in its own right, or could lead to children writing in the role of Little Bear.

Mantle of the Expert – an inquiry-based approach to teaching and learning where children take the role of a group of experts in a particular field. A unit of work organised in this way might last over several sessions and give children the chance to explore a situation and consider the ideas in a text before meeting the text itself.

Text-based example: *The Wonder Garden* by Kristina S Williams and Jenny Broom

The children could take the role of zoologists charged with the responsibility of recording the animals found in various habitats in the book. After receiving their instructions and being divided into groups, the children could explore the different habitats, using the book itself to 'log' the creatures they have seen and some information about them. The teacher could then introduce an element of drama: the habitats themselves are at risk and the zoologists must make a plan to protect the creatures that they have researched.

Tableaux – the children freeze, pausing the action at a key moment of the story. This allows them to think about what is happening to each of the characters in the frame, to think about a particular idea or message can be conveyed or to consider what is happening from different points of view.

Text-based example: *The Adventures of Odysseus* by Hugh Lupton and Daniel Morden

The children could create a series of tableaux to show how Odysseus outwits Polyphemus the Cyclops in the story. Having a series of still images allows the children to think about the relationship between the characters, the organisation of space and the thoughts and motivations of the characters. This might be useful for children's understanding of the story or it might feed into an oral or written retelling of the story.

Teacher in role – the teacher plays a role in the drama, appearing as a character from the story. They might lead the children through the story, ask questions, require help or prompt action through challenges or invitations.

Text-based example: *Clockwork* by Philip Pullman

The teacher could take the role of Karl, asking for the children's advice about whether he should accept Dr Kalmenius' gift: the mechanical Sir Ironsoul. The children could try to persuade 'Karl' to make the right choice, with the teacher-in-role playing devil's advocate and prompting the children to consider other people's points of view.

Thought tracking – while taking part in the drama, children can be asked to freeze. When tapped on the shoulder, they share the thoughts of their character. This can also be done by one child improvising and another standing next to them voicing the character's thoughts.

Text-based example: *The Day the Crayons Quit* by Drew Daywalt and Oliver Jeffers

The children can take the role of the different crayons in the story, and when prompted, share their thoughts with Duncan (another child or the teacher in role). This gives the children the chance to internalise and rehearse the language of the story, perhaps leading into some writing in role as the crayons.

Thought tunnel – the class forms two lines facing each other. One person walks between the lines as each member of the group speaks, giving an opinion, a warning or advice. The children might have a free choice in what they say or be challenged to speak from a particular point of view so that the two sides are giving opposing advice. When the character reaches the end of the alley, they make their decision.

Text-based example: *On Sudden Hill* by Linda Sarah and Benji Davies

After listening to the story, the children can form two lines: one suggesting that Birt should go and join his friends on the hill and another suggesting that he should stay at home. At the end of the tunnel, the child walking can make their decision.

Whoosh – the teacher narrates the story and the children can join in, taking up roles as characters (or even scenery!) and performing them. When the teacher says 'whoosh!', the children return to their seats ready to begin the next section of the drama.

Text-based example: *The Selfish Crocodile* by Faustin Charles

As the teacher reads the story, the children join in, taking the role of the characters. This helps to bring the story to life, making it memorable for children and helping the teacher to see the children's differing interpretations and understanding.

These techniques are all useful within English lessons, but perhaps it is when they are combined that they are most effective. For example, when studying *Oliver Twist*, the children might hot seat the teacher-in-role as Jack Dawkins, the Artful Dodger, before recording their findings as a character on the wall. Or they may Whoosh a version of the *Little Red Riding Hood* to remind them of the traditional version of the story, before meeting the teacher-in-role as the Big Bad Wolf, who goes on to tell them his version, ahead of reading Toby Ford's *The Wolf's Story*.

Why not try?

Children's willingness to suspend their belief and join in with an invented situation, even if they know it is not real, is used by many teachers both in drama sessions and across the wider curriculum. Investigative approaches making use of The Mantle of the Expert or using a puppet to teach a tricky concept are popular in many

(continued)

Why not try? (*continued*)

primary classrooms. This idea of introducing another character, often one who needs the help of the children, can be a powerful tool in motivating and explaining concepts to children. Another option is to make use of an IWB. Slides or pages can be pre-loaded with comments that can act as a character for the teacher and class to interact with.

For example, the whiteboard might be the voice of Zeus, setting a challenge for a group of brave heroes, or a computer reporting a strange anomaly as part of a drama set in space.

Bibliography

Winston, J. and Tandy, M. (1998) *Beginning Drama 4–11*. London: David Fulton.

Literature

A Friend for Little Bear by Harry Horse
Clockwork by Philip Pullman
Flannan Isle by Wilfred Wilson Gibson
Goldilocks and the Three Bears
Oliver Twist by Charles Dickens
On Sudden Hill by Linda Sarah and Benji Davies
Shakespeare Stories by Leon Garfield
The Adventures of Odysseus by Hugh Lupton and Daniel Morden
The Day the Crayons Quit by Drew Daywalt and Oliver Jeffers
The Lighthouse Keeper's Lunch by Rhonda and David Armitage
The Selfish Crocodile by Faustin Charles
The Wolf's Story by Toby Ford and Izhar Cohen
The Wonder Garden by Kristina S Williams and Jenny Broom

Multimedia and film texts

Developing visual literacy

The nature of the texts children read and interact with has changed greatly in recent times. While a printed text on a page might still be the text that children encounter most at school, developments in technology mean that these texts are increasingly likely to be multimodal – many texts now draw on images, different fonts, diagrams and imaginative layouts to share meaning with their reader. Away from the classroom, images, television, film and interactive online texts such as computer games and websites are likely to form a significant part of a child's wider experiences of texts (Clark, 2016). Even very young children arrive at school having had significant experience of media and digital technologies (Bearne *et al.*, 2007). Perhaps it is not surprisingly that:

> Children's basic understanding of the 'language' of television develops at a very young age. The fundamental 'vocabulary' of camera movements and positions, shot transitions and editing conventions is fairly well-understood by most children by the age of four or five.
>
> (Buckingham, 2005)

While building an understanding of, and being able to create, these texts often relies on traditional literacy skills – read and writing– other forms of literacy are also important in the modern world. Reading and writing using different multimedia, producing work for different audiences and using images and sound in addition to written or spoken language all requires a different range of skills and understanding: in effect, different literacies. The dominant and recurring term amongst the modes of literacy proposed in research is 'visual literacy'. Brill, Kim and Branch (2001) define visual literacy as:

> A group of acquired competencies for interpreting and composing visible messages. A visually literate person is able to:
>
> • Discriminate, and make sense of visible objects as part of a visual acuity
> • Create static and dynamic visible objects effectively in a defined space
> • Comprehend and appreciate the visual testaments of others
> • Conjure objects in the mind's eye
>
> (in Sims *et al.*, 2002)

In most genres of film individual images build to form scenes that, in turn, form a narrative. While it is more common to refer to 'watching a film', the term 'read' can be used to refer to the process of taking meaning from both written and film texts, however film and visual texts have a language of their own (Sefton-Green, 1998). While building an understanding of and being able to create these texts often relies on traditional literacy skills, developing other forms of literacy are also important in the modern world.

The popularity of television and devices for accessing the internet and games presents a challenge to the amount of time children spend reading, but this also presents an opportunity for teachers. If children live in a world of multimedia texts and arrive in the classroom with experience and understanding of film texts, then a text-based curriculum should reflect that. Developing visual literacy and an understanding of multimedia texts doesn't need to come at the expense of traditional reading and writing. Instead, it can support it. Rich film texts can be challenging and motivating for children, providing an immediately accessible catalyst for discussions without the possible barrier of word-reading, just as listening to a book being read aloud can. This chapter considers the role film, digital and multimedia texts can play in developing children's visual literacy, but also the development of their wider reading and writing through considering:

- Film and comprehension
- Films as a scaffold for writing
- Creating film texts
- Films of books as 'the definitive version' of a story

Film and comprehension

Language comprehension is a wider field than reading comprehension, encompassing texts being read aloud and those watched on screen. As a result, film texts can be useful ways of developing children's language comprehension. The process of constructing a mental model of the text is different in a visual medium such as film. Here children are not decoding words on page and using these to construct understanding, instead drawing meaning from images, sounds and the movement of the camera. While the codes are different (perhaps more similar to making meaning from a picturebook), readers draw on the same key strategies to understand these texts (Marsh and Millard, 2000). The key approaches to using a film text for comprehension teaching will be similar to those used with a written text, although the grammar and syntax of film is different.

The same factors for comprehension that we considered in Chapter 4 are relevant for making meaning here:

- Background knowledge
- Vocabulary development
- Inference
- Comprehension monitoring
- Text structure

Film is especially useful as a medium for helping children to be aware of their own understanding (comprehension monitoring) and as a vehicle for children to discuss and ask and answer questions, developing their ability to make inferences. The same key teaching approaches of modelling reading and using questions to drive rich discussion from Chapter 5 apply to film. These teaching approaches will also help to develop children's awareness and understanding of visual literacy too.

The British Film Institute's Primary Education Working Group suggest a number of teaching techniques for making use of film (BFI, 2003). Of those, three are particularly useful for developing children's wider language comprehension:

Freeze frame – the individual elements of a still or short extract of a film can be analysed and discussed in a similar way to a piece of written text. The group might discuss how the elements of the image are positioned in the frame; how the camera angle affects meaning; how lighting and colour create mood; and how movement of the camera carries meaning – zooming in or panning across a scene.

Sound and image – attention is paid specifically to the soundtrack: music, sound effects, spoken words and use of silence. The children might consider how what they hear sets the mood of a text and how sounds share narrative information.

Generic translation – children are challenged to translate the narrative or scene from a moving-image text to a written form, such as a story or newspaper report.

You can find the full document, full of practical advice by searching online for 'BFI look again'.

Think and reflect

While film texts can provide a useful and motivating medium for teaching comprehension and can help to build visual literacy, they are not a like-for-like replacement for reading written texts. The process of building understanding from a film text is different to

(continued)

> **Think and reflect** (*continued*)
>
> that of creating a mental model from reading written words. We should be cautious about generalising the skills and assuming that practising comprehension with texts from one medium will automatically result in an improvement in comprehension in another medium. Film texts can play an important role in a rich text-based curriculum, and high-quality films and moving image texts are valuable to study in their own right, but it is through reading books and other written texts and then thinking about and discussing them that we can primarily help children to become fluent readers.

Films as a scaffold for writing

Deployed thoughtfully, films can support many aspects of writing. In the words of Parker and Pearce (2002), films can 'offer a cradle to support the development of different, yet related, concepts'. A short film can be used to model the structure of a narrative, so children can see how a story builds from beginning, to climax, to resolution. Watching a scene in depth can teach children how a writer can depict a character through his actions rather than describing him explicitly – the 'show, don't tell' method that is a mark of mature narrative writing. The visual nature of film can support children's descriptive writing. Having something concrete to see helps children to concentrate on the language they use and the images they create in their writing, rather than having to both invent the scene *and* represent it in writing.

There are many wonderful standalone films that can be used as a scaffold for structuring writing. These can be found by searching the many sites online that host films suitable for primary schools. Through showing children a film and then discussing it, we can scaffold children's understanding of the story. Of course the images don't have to move. Photographs, drawings or wordless picturebooks such as *Journey* by Aaron Becker or *The Mysteries of Harris Burdick* by Chris Van Allsburg can make useful scaffolds for writing.

Why not try?

Five wonderful films for scaffolding writing:

- *Shakespeare: The Animated Tales* (1992, S4C/BBC)
- *Paperman* (2012, Disney Shorts)
- *Piper* (2016, Pixar Shorts)
- *The Lighthouse* (2016, Simon Scheiber)
- British Pathé news reels (such as Neil Armstrong walking on the moon or Emily Davison throwing herself under the King's horse) (Various, British Pathé)

Each of these can be found by searching online or you can browse a selection of films by age or topic at www.filmclub.org/films.

Creating film texts

If a text-based curriculum is to truly embrace the texts that children encounter in the modern world, then producing film texts as well as reading them should feature. While the skills and knowledge involved in this are likely to be outside the range of a national curriculum, film-making can be a valuable exercise. Parallels can be drawn between film-making and the planning–creating–editing process of writing (although making a film is a time-consuming way of teaching this and the skills may not be readily transferable), but the value lies in the creative process itself, with children involved in an 'imaginative activity fashioned so as to produce outcomes that are both original and of value' (NACCCE, 1999). Film-making based on an existing written text can support children to appreciate and think deeply about a text. An effective model for film-making in the primary classroom might be:

1. Think about the language of film

Begin the unit by showing the class an example of short scene from a film adaptation and compare this with the same part of the story from the original book. As a class, consider some key questions:

- What happens in the scene?
- What is the mood of the scene? Is there a difference between the film and the book?
- How do we know how the main character is feeling? Which words does the book use to show this? How does the film show this?
- How does the film use lighting, sound-effects and music to create a particular atmosphere?

2. Introduce the technology

From video cameras to flip-cams to tablets, there are many devices children can use to create films. The best way for children to develop their skills in this area is to get started; have a go; make some mistakes and then learn from them. However, a session introducing the children to the technology they'll be using and some basics about filming techniques (keeping the camera still, framing shots, thinking about background, even explaining the idea of editing shots together later in the process) can be useful and will help to avoid wasted time later.

3. Plan the film

Working in small groups, the children can now plan their own film. The first step is to create a storyboard for their film, planning the shots they need. Then they need to decide how they will turn their plan into film footage. The questions they might need to consider are:

- Who will be the director and who will act? Who will operate the camera? Who will edit the final film? Or will the roles be shared, with different members of the group taking responsibility for different scenes?
- Do you need a script or will you improvise the scene? Can you use the dialogue from the book or will you need to make changes?
- Will you need to make any special costumes or props?
- Where will you film each scene?
- Will you need to use any music or sound effects?

4. Create and edit the film

Now the groups can begin filming. Once the footage is collected, the children can use software to edit their film and add any music or sound-effects. It also gives them an opportunity to add post-production effects such as titles, a soundtrack or even to make use of the special-effects that are part of most editing software.

Why not try?

Sharing book trailers – Book trailers are now created for many children's books. While these short and exciting films are often commercial creations intended to sell the book, they can be a useful way of introducing children to different books and generating a sense of excitement about reading them. Many book trailers can be found by searching online. The Blue Peter Book Award (again, search online) also features attractive animated book trailers for each of the shortlisted books.

(continued)

> **Why not try?** (*continued*)
>
> As well as watching book trailers, making film trailers for the books the children read can be very motivating. One successful approach is for children to read a book in small-group reading and then create a book trailer of what they have read. This helps them to picture the scene in their imagination as they read and can be a motivating outcome after reading the novel itself.

Films of books as 'the definitive version' of a story

While films can be a motivating hook for writing and can also be a useful way of communicating a story which children can then discuss, we need to be cautious about sharing films of a book with children before they have read the written text. Once children have seen the film version, very often this will become their definitive version: when they imagine the story or the characters, they will see the images from the film version, rather than their own imagination. This is not simply an issue because part of the joy of reading is that each reader imagines a slightly different version of the story, and watching a film version first prevents that happening. It also prevents a child from having the chance to construct a mental model based on the words they read, depriving them of valuable practice of this key skill.

There are reasons why watching a film version of a written text can be useful, however. If the film version is a faithful adaptation, then watching a film gives children a clear idea of what the text is about – both what happens in the scene and the intended effect on the audience. Equipped with this shared understanding, the children can then consider the written text and analyse it to see how the author creates these same effects through written language. With *The Wind in the Willows* for example, watching a film version of the scene where Mole ventures into the Wild Wood (see Chapter 9), the children can see that Mole is scared and confused through his actions and the grammar of the film. When they read the text itself, they know what the intended effect on the reader is (empathy with Mole's situation and to communicate his distress) and they can then move straight to seeing how the author does this through choice of language features and the organisation of the text – in this case, through variety of sentence structure and grammatical construction.

What is important is that watching the film version is a conscious decision by the teacher to support a specific teaching point. Sometimes this option will not be available to the teacher. Part of the reality of teaching in the 21st-century is that children will have already have seen film versions of many of the literary heritage stories encountered, especially fairy stories and popular films adapted from classic children's literature such as *Alice's Adventures in Wonderland*, *Peter Pan* or *The Jungle Book*. This provides a challenge as children may feel they know the 'real' version of the story and that a written text, which may be very different, might be viewed as 'wrong', even if it is the original version of the story. This also provides an opportunity to discuss different adaptations of the same story, which draw out different themes and ideas. This is especially true of traditional tales and fairy stories which have their origins in oral tales, passed from person to person. Exploring the differences between different versions of a story enables considered conversations about audience and purpose and the differences between texts on screen and on the page.

In summary

- Film and multimodal texts play an increasingly important part in children's developing literacy; visual literacy is important to make meaning from these texts

- Film can be useful for teaching strands of traditional literacy, although care must be taken not to overgeneralise the skills children are using so that film is seen as a like-for-like replacement for a written text

- Many children will be familiar with versions of traditional stories or children's literature from popular films. This needs to be acknowledged and can provide an opportunity to discuss different versions of the same story

Bibliography

Bearne, E., Clark, C., Johnson, A., Manford, P., Motram, M. and Wolstencroft, H., with Anderson, R., Gamble, N. and Overall, L. (2007) *Reading on Screen: Research Report*. Leicester: UKLA.

BFI Primary Education Working Group (2003) *Look Again!: A Teaching Guide to Using Film and Television with Three-to Eleven-Year Olds*. London: DfES.

Brill, J. M., Kim, D. and Branch, R. M. (2001) Visual literacy defined: the results of a Delphi study – can IVLA (operationally) define visual literacy? In R. E. Griffen, V. S. Williams and J. Lee (eds) *Exploring the Visual Future: Art Design, Science and Technology* (pp. 9–15). Blacksburg, VA: The International Visual Literacy Association.

Buckingham, D. (2005) *The Media Literacy of Children and Young People: A Review of the Research Literature on Behalf of Ofcom*. London: London Knowledge Lab.

Clark, C. (2016) *Children's and Young People's Reading in 2015. Findings from the 2015 National Literacy Trust's Annual Survey*. London: National Literacy Trust.

Kress, G. and van Leeuwen, T. (2006) *The Grammar of Visual Design*. Routledge: London.

Marsh, J. and Millard, E. (2000) *Literacy and Popular Culture: Using Children's Culture in the Classroom*. London: Chapman.

NACCCE (1999) *All Our Futures: Creativity, Culture & Education*. London: HMSO.

Parker, D. and Pearce, H. (2002) *Story Shorts – Using Film to Teach Literacy*. London: DfES.

Sefton-Green, J. (ed) (1998) *Digital Diversions: Young Culture in the Age of Multimedia*. London: UCL Press.

Sims, E., O'Leary, R., Cook, J. and Butland, G. (2002) *Visual Literacy: What Is It and Do We Need It to Use Learning Technologies Effectively?* Sydney: ASCILITE conference proceedings.

Literature

Journey by Aaron Becker
The Mysteries of Harris Burdick by Chris Van Allsburg
The Wind in the Willows by Kenneth Grahame

Appendix I

Text-based
curriculum map

This map outlines the texts that will be taught in English lessons, covering the teaching of reading, writing and spoken language. In addition to this, children will be taught specific aspects of English through small group reading, independent reading, listening to books read aloud, phonics teaching and discrete spelling and handwriting lessons.

English – Year 1

Unit	Example texts	Ongoing outcomes	Writing for purpose	Ongoing language teaching
Classic tales (4 x 1–2 weeks)	Traditional tales, told or read, including: *Little Red Riding Hood* *Goldilocks and the Three Bears* *The Gingerbread Man* *The Billy Goats Gruff* *The Magic Porridge Pot* *Cinderella* *Snow White* *Hansel and Gretel* *Jack and the Beanstalk* *Nosy Crow Fairy Tales Apps* And stories derived from them, for example *Little Red Riding Hood*: *Good Little Wolf* by Nadia Shireen *The Wolf's Story* by Toby Forward	Oral retellings of stories Book reviews or personal responses Character studies Drama and role-play	**Entertain:** Simple narrative – retelling a traditional tale or imitating a story but with changes, such as *Tom and the Three Wolves* or *The Magic Hot Chocolate Cup* **Describe:** Detailed description of one setting from a text (the forest, a witch's gingerbread house, the giant's castle)	Joining **words** and **sentences** using *and* How the **prefix** *un-* changes the meaning of **verbs** and **adjectives** (negation, e.g. *unkind, untie the boat*) Regular **plural noun suffixes** *-s* or *-es* (e.g. *dog, dogs; wish, wishes*) **Suffixes** that can be added to **verbs** (e.g. *helping, helped, helper*) How **words** can combine to make **sentences** Sequencing **sentences** to form short narratives Separation of **words** with spaces Introduction to capital letters, full stops, question marks and exclamation marks to demarcate **sentences** Capital letters for names and for the personal **pronoun** *I*
Well-loved Stories (4 x 1–2 weeks)	*The Very Hungry Caterpillar* by Eric Carle *Where the Wild Things Are* by Maurice Sendak *We're Going on a Bearhunt* by Michael Rosen *The Tiger Who Came to Tea* by Judith Kerr *Not Now, Bernard* by David McKee	Oral retellings of stories Book reviews or personal responses Character studies Drama and role-play	**Entertain:** Simple narrative – retelling a story or imitating story but with changes, such as *The Elephant Who Came to Tea* or *We're Going on a Bearhunt* but with different obstacles	

English – Year 1 (continued)

Unit	Example texts	Ongoing outcomes	Writing for purpose	Ongoing language teaching
	Would You Rather . . . by John Burningham *Owl Babies* by Martin Waddell *Rosie's Walk* by Pat Hutchins *Mr Gumpy's Outing* by John Burningham *Hairy Maclary* by Lynley Dodd		**Describe:** Detailed description of a character from the story – the monster that Bernard meets or Bill from *Owl Babies* **Inform:** A short non-fiction text about an element of one of the books: the life-cycle of a caterpillar or owls and their habitat	
Contemporary picture-books (4 × 1–2 weeks)	*Oh No, George!* by Chris Haughton *Lost and Found* by Oliver Jeffers *Oi Frog!* and *Oi Dog!* by Kes Gray and Jim Field *Open Very Carefully* by Nick Bromley *Puffin Peter* by Petr Horacek *The Crocodile Who Didn't Like Water* by Gemma Merino *A Friend for Little Bear* by Harry Horse	Oral retellings of stories Book reviews or personal responses Character studies Drama and role-play	**Entertain:** Simple narrative – retelling a story or imitating story but with changes to characters or their adventures or a new story starring a character they have met in a book Extra pages – writing additional pages for books (for example, extra animals for *Oi Frog!* – 'armadillos sit on pillows' etc.). Diary – a character's diary telling the story from their point of view (e.g. Little Bear or the penguin from *Lost and Found*). **Describe:** Detailed description of a character from the story – George or Puffin Peter.	

(Continued)

English – Year 1 (continued)

Unit	Example texts	Ongoing outcomes	Writing for purpose	Ongoing language teaching
Poetry (3 x 1 week)	A broad range of different types of poems from: *Michael Rosen's A–Z of Children's Poetry* by Michael Rosen *101 Poems for Children* by Carol Anne Duffy *The Nation's Favourite Children's Poems* *iF Poems* (as a book or app) Different types of poems, including: Acrostic poems Calligrams/shape poems	Personal response/ book review Performance of poem	**Entertain:** Write own poems based on existing poems (e.g. a poem about water or mud based on *Sand* by John Foster or based on a poem with a clear setting such as *Down Behind the Dustbins* by Michael Rosen)	
Poetry (1 week)	Children's own choice of poem	Performance of poem Hand-written version of poem for class anthology	**Persuade:** Short comment to accompany chosen poem explaining why everyone should read it	
Non-fiction (3 x 2 weeks)	Range of high quality non-fiction (both books and online/apps) linked to wider topic/foundation subjects	Book reviews or personal responses Summary of facts learnt	**Inform:** Pages of non-fiction books linked to topic studied and based on books that have been read	
Instruc-tions (2 x 1 week)	Recipes or instructions from real-life or drawn from a text (e.g. *Mr Wolf's Pancakes* by Jan Fernley)	Oral instructions and directions	**Instruct:** Writing instructions linked to real-life experiences or from a situation in a book **Instruct:** Directions using map of local area or from a book	

English – Year 1 (continued)

Unit	Example texts	Ongoing outcomes	Writing for purpose	Ongoing language teaching
Recounts (ongoing)	Linked to educational visits and visitors to school/workshops or from imaginative work in drama		**Inform:** Recounts from real experiences or imagined worlds of drama	

English – Year 2

Unit	Example texts	Ongoing outcomes	Writing for purpose	Ongoing language teaching
Classic tales (3 x 1–2 weeks)	Stories from *Fairy Tales* told by Berlie Doherty *Aladdin and the Enchanted Lamp* retold by Philip Pullman Stories from *A River of Stories* compiled by Alice Curry and Jan Pienkowski *Dragon Mountain* by Tim Vyner *The Brave Sister* retold by Fiona Waters *Selkie* by Gillan McClure	Oral retellings of stories Book reviews or personal responses Character studies Drama and role-play	**Entertain:** Simple narrative – retelling a traditional tale or imitating story but with changes, such as another story featuring Selkies or another adventure of Aladdin **Describe:** Detailed description of one setting from a text (Dragon Mountain, the Scottish coast) **Inform:** A short non-fiction text about a country or time in history from one of the books studied	Revision/consolidation of Y1 Objectives And: Formation of **nouns** using **suffixes** such as -*ness*, -*er* Formation of **adjectives** using **suffixes** such as -*ful*, -*less* (a fuller list of **suffixes** can be found in the Year 2 spelling appendix) Use of the **suffixes** -*er* and -*est* to form comparisons of **adjectives** and **adverbs** **Subordination** (using *when*, *if*, *that*, or *because*) and **co-ordination** (using *or*, *and* or *but*) Expanded **noun phrases** for description and specification (e.g. *the blue butterfly, plain flour, the man in the moon*) **Sentences** with different forms: statement, question, exclamation, command Correct choice and consistent use of **present tense and past tense** throughout writing

(Continued)

English – Year 2 (continued)

Unit	Example texts	Ongoing outcomes	Writing for purpose	Ongoing language teaching
				Use of the **continuous** form of **verbs** in the **present** and **past tense** to mark actions in progress (e.g. *she is drumming, be was shouting*) Use of capital letters, full stops, question marks and exclamation marks to demarcate **sentences** Commas to separate items in a list **Apostrophes** to mark contracted forms in spelling
Picture-books (3 x 1–2 weeks)	*Peace at Last* by Jill Murphy *The Lighthouse Keeper's Lunch* by Rhonda and David Armitage *Dogger* by Shirley Hughes *Courtney* by John Burningham *The Selfish Crocodile* by Faustin Charles *The Jolly Postman* by Janet and Alan Ahlberg *The Forest Child* by Richard Edwards *Beegu* by Alexis Deacon *Traction Man is Here* by Mini Grey	Oral retellings of stories Book reviews or personal responses Character studies Drama and role-play	**Entertain:** Simple narrative – retelling a story or imitating a story but with changes, such a story about a lost toy, using the structure of *Dogger*, or a story about a visitor from space such as Beegu Letters – letters from characters in the stories to one another or using text as a model (e.g. *The Jolly Postman*) **Describe:** Detailed description of a character from the story (e.g. the Selfish Crocodile or Courtney).	

English – Year 2 (continued)

Unit	Example texts	Ongoing outcomes	Writing for purpose	Ongoing language teaching
Books by well-known authors (2 x 2 weeks)	Anthony Brown Shirley Hughes Janet and Alan Ahlberg Quentin Blake John Burningham Mini Grey	Discussions around themes or ideas that are shared across different books Book reviews or personal responses Character studies Drama and role-play	**Entertain:** Simple narrative – retelling a story or imitating story but with changes to characters or their adventures or a new story starring a character they have met in a book 'Missing book' – writing a new book in the style of the author studied **Inform:** A short biography of the author studied	
Longer narratives (2 x 2–3 weeks)	*Flat Stanley* by Jeff Brown *Mango and Bambang* by Polly Faber and Clara Vulliamy *Pugs of the Frozen North* by Philip Reeve and Sarah McIntyre *The Twits* by Roald Dahl *George's Marvellous Medicine* by Roald Dahl	Oral retellings of stories Book reviews or personal responses Character studies Drama and role-play	**Entertain:** Simple narrative – telling a story starring the characters from the book studied (Mango and Bambang's next adventure) Simple narrative – another story with a similar theme (a first-person story about a magical potion and what it did) Simple narrative – an extra chapter for a book (e.g. what happened to Mugglewump and his family next or another adventure for Shen and Sika) Diary – a character's diary telling the story from their point of view (e.g. Shen or George's Grandma)	

(Continued)

English – Year 2 (continued)

Unit	Example texts	Ongoing outcomes	Writing for purpose	Ongoing language teaching
			Describe: Detailed description of a setting from the story (e.g. the frozen North Pole or the city); or description of a character (Mr Twit or Stanley)	
Poetry (3 x 1 week)	A broad range of different types of poems from: *Michael Rosen's A–Z of Children's Poetry* by Michael Rosen / *101 Poems for Children* by Carol Anne Duffy / *The Nation's Favourite Children's Poems* / *iF Poems* (as a book or app) / Different types of poems, including: Acrostic poems / Calligrams/shape poems / Haiku / Kennings	Personal response/ book review / Performance of poem	**Entertain:** Write own poems based on existing poems (e.g. a poem about colours based on *What is Pink?* by Christina Rossetti or a poem using nonsense words based on *On the Ning Nang Nong* by Spike Milligan)	
Poetry (1 week)	Children's own choice of poem	Performance of poem / Hand-written version of poem for class anthology	**Persuade:** Short comment to accompany chosen poem explaining why everyone should read it	

English – Year 2 (continued)

Unit	Example texts	Ongoing outcomes	Writing for purpose	Ongoing language teaching
Non-fiction (3 x 2 weeks)	Range of high quality non-fiction (both books and online/apps) linked to wider topic/foundation subjects	Book reviews or personal responses\ Summary of facts learnt	**Inform:** Pages of non-fiction books linked to topic studied and based on books that have been read	
Instructions (1 week)	Recipes or instructions from real-life or drawn from a non-fiction text	Oral instructions and directions	**Instruct:** Writing instructions linked to real-life experiences or from a situation in a book **Instruct:** Directions using map of local area or from a book (such as *Maps* by Aleksandra and Daniel Mizielinski)	
Recounts (ongoing)	Linked to educational visits and visitors to school/workshops or from imaginative work in drama		**Inform:** Recounts from real experiences or imagined worlds of drama	

(Continued)

English – Year 3

Unit	Example texts	Ongoing outcomes	Writing for purpose	English-language opportunities	Ongoing language teaching
Classic narratives (2 x 2–3 weeks)	**The Odyssey** *The Adventures of Odysseus* by Hugh Lupton and Daniel Morden *The Odyssey* retold by Robin Lister *The Iliad and The Odyssey* retold by Marcia Williams **Sinbad the Sailor** *The Seven Voyages of Sinbad the Sailor* by John Yeoman **Myths from Across the World** *Myths and Legends* by Anthony Horowitz *Robin Hood and a World of Other Stories* by Geraldine McCaughrean	Oral retellings of stories Book reviews or personal responses Character studies Drama and role-play	**Entertain:** Extended narrative – retelling the story as first-person narrative, with own adventures Diary – a character's diary telling the story from their point of view (e.g. Odysseus or Sinbad) Letters – letters from characters in the stories to one another (Penelope or Telemachus to Odysseus) **Describe:** Detailed description of one setting from a text (The Island of the Lotus Eaters or the City of Troy) **Inform:** A short non-fiction text about a country or time in history from one of the books studied	Inverted commas to punctuate direct speech Expressing time and cause using **conjunctions** (e.g. when, so, before, after, while, because); adverbs (e.g. before, after, during, because of) or prepositions (e.g. before, after, during, in, because of)	Formation of nouns using a range of prefixes such as *super-, anti-, auto-* Use of the determiners *a* or *an* according to whether the next word begins with a consonant or a vowel Using paragraphs as a way to group related material Headings and subheadings to aid presentation Use of the perfect form of verbs to mark relationships of time and cause Inverted commas to punctuate direct speech
Narrative texts (2 x 3 weeks)	*The Last Polar Bears* by Harry Horse *Clockwork* by Philip Pullman *The Firework-Maker's Daughter* by Philip Pullman	Oral retellings of stories Book reviews or personal responses	**Entertain:** Extended narrative – story using structure of the book studied (a quest such as *The Firework-Maker's Daughter* or a story within a story in *Clockwork*)	Inverted commas to punctuate direct speech	

English – Year 3 (continued)

Unit	Example texts	Ongoing outcomes	Writing for purpose	English-language opportunities	Ongoing language teaching
		Character studies Drama and role-play	Diary – a character's diary telling the story from their point of view (e.g. Lila or Roo) Letters – narrative told as series of letters from characters in the stories (as Grandfather does in *The Last Polar Bears*) **Describe:** Detailed description of one character from a text (e.g. Lila or Doctor Kalmenius)	Expressing time and cause using **conjunctions** (e.g. when, so, before, after, while, because); adverbs (e.g. before, after, during, because of) or prepositions (e.g. before, after, during, in, because of)	
Picture-books (2 x 1–2 weeks)	*Tuesday* by David Wiesner *On Sudden Hill* by Linda Sarah and Benji Davies *Grandad's Island* by Benji Davies *Weasels* by Elys Dolan	Oral retellings of stories- Book reviews or personal responses Character studies Drama and role-play	**Entertain:** Narrative – retelling a story from a different character's point of view (e.g. the Gargoyles or the detective in *Tuesday*) Narrative – using wordless picturebook as frame for writing own narrative Narrative – creating own 3-page picturebook, using illustrations and text to tell story	Inverted commas to punctuate direct speech Expressing time and cause using **conjunctions** (e.g. when, so, before, after, while, because); adverbs (e.g. before, after, during, because of) or prepositions (e.g. before, after, during, in, because of)	

(Continued)

English – Year 3 (continued)

Unit	Example texts	Ongoing outcomes	Writing for purpose	English-language opportunities	Ongoing language teaching
Well-loved narratives (3–4 weeks)	*Just So Stories* by Rudyard Kipling *How the Whale Became* by Ted Hughes *The Iron Man* by Ted Hughes *The BFG* by Roald Dahl *The Little Prince* by Antoine de Saint-Exupéry	Oral retellings of stories Book reviews or personal responses Character studies Drama and role-play	**Describe:** Detailed description of a setting from the story (e.g. city from the Gargoyles' viewpoint or Fungus' home) **Entertain:** Narrative – writing a missing story from the collection explain how a creature came to be the way it is (based on stories from *Just So Stories* or *How the Whale Became*) Playscript – retelling a story as a playscript (and then performing it) **Inform:** A short non-fiction text about a creature from one of the books studied (e.g. what the rhinoceros or whale are *actually* like)	Inverted commas to punctuate direct speech Expressing time and cause using **conjunctions** (e.g. when, so, before, after, while, because); adverbs (e.g. before, after, during, because of) or prepositions (e.g. before, after, during, in, because of)	
Shakespeare stories (2–3 weeks)	**The Tempest** *Shakespeare Stories* by Leon Garfield *Shakespeare: The Animated Tales*	Oral retellings of stories Drama and role-play	**Discuss:** Character study of one character showing understanding of story and themes **Persuade:** Persuasive essay argument to answer key question from text (e.g. Is Prospero a good father?)	Expressing time and cause using **conjunctions** (e.g. when, so, before, after, while, because); adverbs (e.g. before, after, during, because of) or prepositions (e.g. before, after, during, in, because of)	

English – Year 3 (continued)

Unit	Example texts	Ongoing outcomes	Writing for purpose	English-language opportunities	Ongoing language teaching
				Headings and subheadings to aid presentation	
Non-fiction (2 x 2 weeks)	Range of high quality non-fiction (both books and online/apps) linked to wider topic/foundation subjects	Book reviews or personal responses Summary of new ideas considered/facts learnt	**Inform:** Pages of non-fiction books/webpages linked to topic studied and based on books that have been read	Headings and subheadings to aid presentation	
Biography (1–2 weeks)	Picture book biographies, such as: *Enormous Smallness* by Matthew Burgess (about E. E. Cummings) *On Beam of Light* by Jennifer Berne (about Albert Einstein) *Star Stuff* by Stephanie Roth Sisson (about Carl Sagan) Books from the *Little People, Big Dreams* series (Marie Curie, Maya Angelou or Frida Kahlo, for example)	Book reviews or personal responses Summary of new ideas considered/facts learnt	**Inform:** A short, illustrated biography of a significant character from history, based on research	Using paragraphs as a way to group related material Headings and subheadings to aid presentation	
Instructions (1 week)	Recipes or instructions from real-life or drawn from a text	Oral instructions and directions	**Instruct:** Writing instructions linked to real-life experiences or from situation in a book **Instruct:** Directions using map of local area or from a book	**Instructions** (2 x 1 week)	

(Continued)

English – Year 3 (continued)

Unit	Example texts	Ongoing outcomes	Writing for purpose	English-language opportunities	Ongoing language teaching
Recounts (ongoing)	Linked to educational visits and visitors to school/ workshops or from imaginative work in drama		**Inform:** Recounts from real experiences or imagined worlds of drama	Use of the perfect form of verbs to mark relationships of time and cause	
Poetry (3 x 1 week)	A broad range of different types of poems from: *The Rattle Bag* compiled by Seamus Heaney and Ted Hughes *The Nation's Favourite Children's Poems* *The Ring of Words* edited by Roger McGough *iF Poems* (as a book or app) *Please Mrs Butler* by Alan Ahlberg Different types of poems, including: Narrative poems Calligrams/shape poems Haiku Kennings	Personal response/ book review Performance of poem	**Entertain:** Write own poems based on existing poems (e.g. a narrative poem based on *Adventures of Isobel* by Ogden Nash or a poem set in school, such as those in *Please Mrs Butler*		
Poetry (1 week)	Children's own choice of poem	Performance of poem Hand-written version of poem for class anthology	**Persuade:** Short comment to accompany chosen poem explaining why everyone should read it		

English – Year 4

Unit	Example texts	Ongoing outcomes	Writing for purpose	English-language opportunities	Ongoing language teaching
Classic narratives (2 x 2–3 weeks)	The Labours of Hercules *Greek Heroes* by Geraldine McCaughrean *The Twelve Labours of Hercules* by James Ford *Greek Myths* retold by Marcia Williams Tales from 1001 Nights *One Thousand and One Arabian Nights* retold by Geraldine McCaughrean *The Arabian Nights* by Michael Foreman *The Thousand Nights and One Night* retold by David Walser and Jan Pienkowski	Oral retellings of stories Book reviews or personal responses Character studies Drama and role-play	**Entertain:** Extended narrative – retelling the story as first-person narrative, with own adventures Extended narrative – using story as a frame for own stories (e.g. new stories for Shahrazad to tell) Playscript – retelling a story as a playscript (and then performing it) **Describe:** Detailed description of one character from a text (e.g. Hercules or Shahrazad) **Inform:** A short non-fiction text about a country or time in history from one of the books studied	Standard English forms for verb inflections instead of local spoken forms (e.g. *we were* instead of *we was*, or *I did* instead of *I done*) Use of inverted commas to punctuate direct speech	The grammatical difference between plural and possessive -s Standard English forms for verb inflections instead of local spoken forms (e.g. *we were* instead of *we was*, or *I did* instead of *I did*) Appropriate choice of pronoun or noun within a sentence to avoid ambiguity and repetition Fronted adverbials (e.g. *later that day, I heard the bad news*) Use of paragraphs to organise ideas around a theme Appropriate choice of pronoun or noun across sentences to aid cohesion and avoid repetition Use of inverted commas to punctuate direct speech Apostrophes to mark singular and plural possession (e.g. *the girl's name, the boys' boots*) Use of commas after fronted adverbials

(Continued)

English – Year 4 (continued)

Unit	Example texts	Ongoing outcomes	Writing for purpose	English-language opportunities	Ongoing language teaching
Narrative texts (2 x 3 weeks)	*Kensuke's Kingdom* by Michael Morpurgo *Coraline* by Neil Gaiman *Odd and the Frost Giants* by Neil Gaiman *Diamond Brothers* books by Anthony Horowitz	Oral retellings of stories Book reviews or personal responses Character studies Drama and role-play	**Entertain:** Extended narrative – story using structure of the book studied (a story set on an island such as *Kensuke's Kingdom* or a story set in an alternative world such as *Coraline*) Diary – a character's diary telling the story from their point of view (e.g. Tim Diamond or Coraline) **Describe:** Detailed description of one setting from a text (e.g. Kensuke's island)	Standard English forms for verb inflections instead of local spoken forms (e.g. *we were* instead of *we was*, or *I did* instead of *I done*) Use of inverted commas to punctuate direct speech	
Picture-books and graphic novels (2 x 1–2 weeks)	*Instructions* by Neil Gaiman *Flotsam* by David Weisner *Fungus the Bogeyman* by Raymond Briggs *Night of the Gargoyles* by Eve Bunting *The Cat from Hunger Mountain* by Ed Young	Oral retellings of stories Book reviews or personal responses Character studies Drama and role-play	**Entertain:** Narrative – using wordless picturebook as frame for writing own narrative Narrative – creating own picturebook or graphic novel, using illustrations and text to tell story **Instruct:** Quest written as a set of instructions linked to *Instructions*	Inverted commas to punctuate direct speech	

English – Year 4 (continued)

Unit	Example texts	Ongoing outcomes	Writing for purpose	English-language opportunities	Ongoing language teaching
Well-loved narratives (3–4 weeks)	*Charlotte's Web* by E. B. White *The Wind in the Willows* by Kenneth Grahame	Oral retellings of stories Book reviews or personal responses Character studies Drama and role-play	**Entertain:** Narrative – writing a missing chapter or 'further adventures' of one character (e.g. Mr Toad) Playscript – retelling a story as a playscript (and then performing it) Poem – a poem about one character from the story. **Describe:** Detailed description of one setting from a text (e.g. The Wild Wood or the fair) **Discuss:** Character study of one character showing understanding of story and themes	Use of inverted commas to punctuate direct speech Fronted adverbials (e.g. *later that day, I heard the bad news*) Use of commas after fronted adverbials	
Shakespeare stories (2–3 weeks)	**Macbeth** *Shakespeare Stories* by Leon Garfield *Shakespeare: The Animated Tales* *Stories from Shakespeare* by Geraldine McCaughrean	Oral retellings of stories Drama and role-play	**Discuss:** Character study of one character, showing understanding of story and themes **Persuade:** Persuasive essay argument to answer key question from text (e.g. who is responsible for King Duncan's death?)	Standard English forms for verb inflections instead of local spoken forms (e.g. *we were* instead of *we was*, or *I did* instead of *I done*)	

(Continued)

English – Year 4 (continued)

Unit	Example texts	Ongoing outcomes	Writing for purpose	English-language opportunities	Ongoing language teaching
Non-fiction (2 x 2 weeks)	Range of high quality non-fiction (both books and online/apps) linked to wider topic/foundation subjects	Book reviews or personal responses Summary of new ideas considered/facts learnt	**Inform:** Pages of non-fiction books/webpages linked to topic studied and based on books that have been read	Appropriate choice of pronoun or noun within a sentence to avoid ambiguity and repetition	
Biography (1–2 weeks)	A range of published biographies (books and online) linked to foundation subjects/science	Book reviews or personal responses Summary of new ideas considered/facts learnt	**Inform:** A short, illustrated biography of a significant character from history, based on research	Standard English forms for verb inflections instead of local spoken forms (e.g. *we were* instead of *we was*, or *I did* instead of *I done*)	
Recounts (ongoing)	Linked to educational visits and visitors to school/workshops or from imaginative work in drama		**Inform:** Recounts from real experiences or imagined worlds of drama		
Poetry (3 x 1 week)	A broad range of different types of poems from: *The Rattle Bag* compiled by Seamus Heaney and Ted Hughes	Personal response/book review Performance of poem			

English – Year 4 (continued)

Unit	Example texts	Ongoing outcomes	Writing for purpose	English-language opportunities	Ongoing language teaching
	The Nation's Favourite Children's Poems *The Ring of Words* edited by Roger McGough *iF Poems* (as a book or app) *Please Mrs Butler* by Alan Ahlberg Different types of poems, including: Narrative poems Calligrams/shape poems Haiku Kennings		**Discuss:** Personal responses to a range of poems using different language forms showing understanding of ideas, language and themes (including poems written in different dialects, such as: *Talking Turkeys* by Benjamin Zephaniah or *Don't Call Alligator* . . . by John Agard and older poems such as *Snake* by D. H. Lawrence or *The Eagle* by Alfred, Lord Tennyson) **Entertain:** Write own poems based on existing poems (e.g. a poem about nature using a familiar pattern such as *The Trees Dance* by Libby Houston)	Standard English forms for verb inflections instead of local spoken forms (e.g. *we were* instead of *we was*, or *I did* instead of *I done*)	
Poetry (1 week)	Children's own choice of poem	Performance of poem Hand-written version of poem for class anthology	**Persuade:** Short comment to accompany chosen poem explaining why everyone should read it		

(Continued)

English – Year 5

Unit	Example texts	Ongoing outcomes	Writing for purpose	English-language opportunities	Ongoing language teaching
Classic narratives (2 x 2–3 weeks)	**Robin Hood** *Robin of Sherwood* by Michael Morpurgo **Trickster Tales** *Trick of the Tale* by John and Caitlin Matthews Anansi Stories from *Tales from the West Indies* by Faustin Charles	Oral retellings of stories Book reviews or personal responses Character studies Drama and role-play	**Entertain:** Extended narrative – using story as a frame for own stories (e.g. further adventures for Robin Hood/tricks for Anansi to play) **Discuss:** Character study of one character showing understanding of character and motivations	Devices to build **cohesion** within a paragraph (e.g. *then, after that, this, firstly*) Linking ideas across paragraphs using **adverbials** of time (e.g. *later*), place (e.g. *nearby*) and number (e.g. *secondly*)	Converting **nouns** or **adjectives** into **verbs** using **suffixes** (e.g. *-ate; -ise; -ify*) **Verb prefixes** (e.g. *dis-, de-, mis-, over- and re-*) **Relative clauses** beginning with *who, which, where, why, whose, that*, or an omitted relative pronoun Indicating degrees of possibility using **modal verbs** (e.g. *might, should, will, must*) or **adverbs** (e.g. *perhaps, surely*) Devices to build **cohesion** within a paragraph (e.g. *then, after that, this, firstly*) Linking ideas across paragraphs using **adverbials** of time (e.g. *later*), place (e.g. *nearby*) and number (e.g. *secondly*) Brackets, dashes or commas to indicate parenthesis Use of commas to clarify meaning or avoid ambiguity

English – Year 5 (continued)

Unit	Example texts	Ongoing outcomes	Writing for purpose	English-language opportunities	Ongoing language teaching
Novels (2 x 3 weeks)	*The Graveyard Book* by Neil Gaiman *Coram Boy* by Jamila Gavin *The Miraculous Journey of Edward Tulane* by Kate DiCamillo *The Imaginary* by A. F. Harrold *My Brother's Ghost* by Alan Ahlberg *The Many Worlds of Albie Bright* by Christopher Edge	Oral retellings of stories Book reviews or personal responses Character studies Drama and role-play	**Entertain:** Extended narrative – story using structures, devices or characters from the novel studied (e.g. 'the further adventures of . . .'; another story set in the same world; or a short story around a similar theme) **Discuss:** Personal responses to the novel showing understanding of ideas, language and themes **Describe:** Detailed description of one character from the text	Devices to build **cohesion** within a paragraph (e.g. *then, after that, this, firstly*) Linking ideas across paragraphs using **adverbials** of time (e.g. *later*), place (e.g. *nearby*) and number (e.g. *secondly*)	
Picture-books and graphic novels (2 x 1–2 weeks)	*Hilda and the Troll* by Luke Pearson *FArTHER* by Graham Baker-Smith *Journey* by Aaron Becker *How to Live Forever* by Colin Thompson *Black Dog* by Levi Pinfold *Mr Wuffles* by David Wiesner	Oral retellings of stories Book reviews or personal responses Character studies Drama and role-play	**Entertain:** Narrative – using wordless picturebook as frame for writing own narrative Narrative – creating own picturebook or graphic novel, using illustrations and text to tell story	**Relative clauses** beginning with *who, which, where, why, whose, that,* or an omitted relative pronoun	

(Continued)

Unit	Example texts	Ongoing outcomes	Writing for purpose	English-language opportunities	Ongoing language teaching
Classic novels (3–4 weeks)	*The Hobbit* by J. R. R. Tolkien *The Wolves of Willoughby Chase* by Joan Aiken *The Call of the Wild* by Jack London *Goodnight Mr Tom* by Michelle Magorian *Carrie's War* by Nina Bawden	Oral retellings of stories Book reviews or personal responses Character studies Drama and role-play	**Entertain:** Extended narrative – story using structures, devices or characters from the novel studied (e.g. 'the further adventures of . . .'; another story set in the same world; or a short story around a similar theme) Interview – interview with one significant character in magazine/online format **Discuss:** Personal responses to the story showing understanding of ideas, language and themes. **Describe:** Detailed description of one settings from a text (e.g. the Shire)	Brackets, dashes or commas to indicate parenthesis Use of commas to clarify meaning or avoid ambiguity The difference between vocabulary typical of informal speech and vocabulary appropriate for formal speech and writing (e.g. *said* versus *reported, alleged,* or *claimed* in formal speech or writing)	
Shakespeare stories (2–3 weeks)	**Julius Caesar** *Shakespeare Stories II* by Leon Garfield *Shakespeare: The Animated Tales Stories from Shakespeare* by Geraldine McCaughrean	Oral retellings of stories Drama and role-play	**Discuss:** Character study of one character showing understanding of story and themes **Persuade:** Persuasive essay argument to answer key question from text (e.g. How do Brutus and Mark Antony win over the people of Rome?)	Devices to build **cohesion** within a paragraph (e.g. *then, after that, this, firstly*) Indicating degrees of possibility using **modal verbs** (e.g. *might, should, will, must*) or **adverbs** (e.g. *perhaps, surely*)	

English – Year 5 (continued)

Unit	Example texts	Ongoing outcomes	Writing for purpose	English-language opportunities	Ongoing language teaching
				Linking ideas across paragraphs using **adverbials** of number (e.g. *secondly*)	
Non-fiction (2 x 2 weeks)	Range of high quality non-fiction (both books and online/apps) linked to wider topic/foundation subjects	Book reviews or personal responses Summary of new ideas considered/ facts learnt	**Inform:** Pages of non-fiction books/ webpages linked to topic studied and based on books that have been read	Devices to build **cohesion** within a paragraph (e.g. *then, after that, this, firstly*) Linking ideas across paragraphs using **adverbials** of time (e.g. *later*), place (e.g. *nearby*) and number (e.g. *secondly*)	
Biography (1–2 weeks)	A range of published biographies (books and online) linked to foundation subjects/science	Book reviews or personal responses Summary of new ideas considered/ facts learnt	**Inform:** A short, illustrated biography of a significant person from history, based on research		
Recounts (ongoing)	Linked to educational visits and visitors to school/ workshops or from imaginative work in drama		**Inform:** Recounts from real experiences or imagined worlds of drama		

(Continued)

English – Year 5 (continued)

Unit	Example texts	Ongoing outcomes	Writing for purpose	English-language opportunities	Ongoing language teaching
Poetry (2 x 1 week)	A broad range of different types of poems from: *Classic Poetry* selected by Michael Rosen *Collected Poems for Children* by Ted Hughes *The Rattle Bag* compiled by Seamus Heaney and Ted Hughes *The Oxford Treasury of Classic Poems* iF *Poems* (as a book or app)	Personal response/ book review Performance of poem	**Discuss:** Personal responses to a range of poems using different language forms showing understanding of ideas, language and themes, including: 1. Poems with similar subjects [on the surface at least] (e.g. *The Fish* by Elizabeth Bishop, *Pike* and *Stickleback* by Ted Hughes) 2. Poems with unfamiliar language structures (e.g. *The Raven* by Edgar Allen Poe or *The Tyger* by William Blake)		
Narrative poetry (1–2 weeks)	*Flannan Isle* by Wilfrid Wilson Gibson *The Highwayman* by Alfred Noyes Poems from *Cautionary Tales* by Hilaire Belloc, such as *Jim, who ran away from his nurse and was eaten by a lion* or *Matilda, who told lies, and was burned to death*	Performance of poem Hand-written version of poem for class anthology	**Entertain:** Narrative-writing a prose narrative version of the poem, using figurative and poetic language **Discuss:** Personal responses to a narrative poem showing understanding of ideas, language and themes		

Unit	Example texts	Ongoing outcomes	Writing for purpose	English-language opportunities	Ongoing language teaching
Classic narratives (2 x 2–3 weeks)	**King Arthur** *Gawain and the Green Knight* retold by Philip Reeve *The Sword and the Circle* by Rosemary Sutcliff *The Once and Future King* by T. H. White **Traditional Tales** *Collected Folk Tales* by Alan Garner *The House of Cats* by Maggie Pearson	Oral retellings of stories Book reviews or personal responses Character studies Drama and role-play	**Entertain:** Extended narrative – using story as a frame for own stories (e.g. further adventures for Knights of the Round Table) **Discuss:** Character study of one character showing understanding of character and motivations Personal responses to the story showing understanding of ideas, language and themes	Use of expanded noun phrases to convey complicated information concisely Differences between vocabulary typical of informal speech and vocabulary appropriate for formal speech and writing (e.g. *said* versus *reported*, *alleged*, or *claimed* in formal speech or writing)	Differences between vocabulary typical of informal speech and vocabulary appropriate for formal speech and writing (e.g. *said* versus *reported*, *alleged* or *claimed* in formal speech or writing) Learn some of the differences between structures typical of informal speech and structures appropriate for formal speech and writing (such as the use of question tags, e.g. *he's your friend, isn't he?*, or the use of the subjunctive in some very formal writing and speech) Use of the semi-colon, colon and dash to mark the boundary between independent clauses (e.g. It's raining; I'm fed up) Use of the colon to introduce a list Hyphens used to avoid ambiguity (e.g. *man eating shark* versus *man-eating shark*, or *recover* versus *re-cover*)

(Continued)

English – Year 6 (continued)

Unit	Example texts	Ongoing outcomes	Writing for purpose	English-language opportunities	Ongoing language teaching
Novels (2 x 4 weeks)	*Rooftoppers* by Katherine Rundell *Freak the Mighty* by Rodman Philbrick *Wonder* by R. J. Palaciao *Raymie Nightingale* by Kate DiCamillo *The Girl of Ink and Stars* by Kiran Millwood Hargrave *Fly by Night* by Frances Hardinge *Northern Lights* by Philip Pullman	Oral retellings of stories Book reviews or personal responses Character studies Drama and role-play	**Entertain:** Extended narrative – story using structures, devices or characters from the novel studied (e.g. 'the further adventures of . . .'; another story set in the same world; or a short story around a similar theme) Letters – from one character to another (Lyra to Iorek or messages between Raymie, Beverly and Elefante) **Discuss:** Personal responses to the novel showing understanding of ideas, language and themes Character study of one character showing understanding of character and motivations	Use of expanded noun phrases to convey complicated information concisely Learn some of the differences between structures typical of informal speech and structures appropriate for formal speech and writing (such as the use of question tags, e.g. *He's your friend, isn't he?*, or the use of the subjunctive in some very formal writing and speech)	

Unit	Example texts	Ongoing outcomes	Writing for purpose	English-language opportunities	Ongoing language teaching
Picture-books and graphic novels (2 x 1–2 weeks)	*The Watertower* by Gary Crew and Steven Woolman *The Island* by Armin Greder *The Mysteries of Harris Burdick* by Chris van Allsburg *The Rabbits* by John Marsden and Shaun Tan *The Arrival* by Shaun Tan	Oral retellings of stories Book reviews or personal responses Character studies Drama and role-play	**Entertain:** Narrative – using wordless picture-book as frame for writing own narrative Narrative – creating own picturebook or graphic novel, using illustrations and text to tell story **Discuss:** Personal responses to the novel showing understanding of ideas, language and themes	Use of expanded noun phrases to convey complicated information concisely	
Classic novels (1 x 3–4 weeks)	*Treasure Island* by Robert Louis Stevenson *Watership Down* by Richard Adams *The Weirdstone of Brisingamen* by Alan Garner *The Wizard of Earthsea* by Ursula Le Guin	Oral retellings of stories Book reviews or personal responses Character studies Drama and role-play	**Entertain:** Extended narrative – story using structures, devices or characters from the novel studied (e.g. 'the further adventures of . . .'; another story set in the same world; or a short story around a similar theme)	Use of the passive voice to affect the presentation of information in a sentence	

(Continued)

English – Year 6 (continued)

Unit	Example texts	Ongoing outcomes	Writing for purpose	English-language opportunities	Ongoing language teaching
			Interview – interview with one significant character in magazine/online format **Discuss:** Personal responses to the story showing understanding of ideas, language and themes	Linking ideas across paragraphs using a wider range of cohesive devices: semantic cohesion (e.g. repetition of a word or phrase), grammatical connections (e.g. the use of adverbials such as *on the other hand, in contrast,* or *as a consequence*) and ellipses Use of different layout devices, such as headings, sub-headings, columns, bullets or tables, to structure text Use the punctuation of bullet points to list information	
Shake-speare stories (2–3 weeks)	**Henry V** *Stories from Shake-speare* by Geraldine McCaughrean	Oral retellings of stories Drama and role-play	**Discuss:** Character study of one character showing under-standing of story and themes	To use expanded noun phrases to convey complicated information concisely	

English – Year 6 (continued)

Unit	Example texts	Ongoing outcomes	Writing for purpose	English-language opportunities	Ongoing language teaching
			Persuade: Speech to motivate an army ready for battle Persuasive essay argument to answer key question from text (e.g. what makes Henry V a good leader?)	Linking ideas across paragraphs using a wider range of cohesive devices: semantic cohesion (e.g. repetition of a word or phrase), grammatical connections (e.g. the use of adverbials such as *on the other hand*, *in contrast*, or *as a consequence*) and ellipses Use the punctuation of bullet points to list information	
Non-fiction (2 x 2 weeks)	Range of high quality non-fiction (both books and online/apps) linked to wider topic/foundation subjects	Book reviews or personal responses Summary of new ideas considered/facts learnt	**Inform:** Pages of non-fiction books/webpages linked to topic studied and based on books that have been read	Use of the colon to introduce a list Hyphens used to avoid ambiguity (e.g. *man eating shark* versus *man-eating shark*, or *recover* versus *re-cover*)	

(Continued)

English – Year 6 (continued)

Unit	Example texts	Ongoing outcomes	Writing for purpose	English-language opportunities	Ongoing language teaching
Biography (1–2 weeks)	A range of published biographies (books and online) linked to foundation subjects/science	Book reviews or personal responses Summary of new ideas considered/facts learnt	**Inform:** A short, illustrated biography of a significant person from history, based on research	Use of expanded noun phrases to convey complicated information concisely	
Recounts (ongoing)	Linked to educational visits and visitors to school/workshops or from imaginative work in drama		**Inform:** Recounts from real experiences or imagined worlds of drama	Linking ideas across paragraphs using a wider range of cohesive devices: semantic cohesion (e.g. repetition of a word or phrase), grammatical connections (e.g. the use of adverbials such as *on the other hand*, *in contrast*, or *as a consequence*) and ellipses	
Poetry (2 x 1 week)	A broad range of different types of poems from: *Classic Poetry* selected by Michael Rosen *The Rattle Bag* compiled by Seamus Heaney and Ted Hughes	Personal response/ book review Performance of poem	**Discuss:** Personal responses to a range of poems using different language forms showing understanding of ideas, language and themes, including:		

English – Year 6 (continued)

Unit	Example texts	Ongoing outcomes	Writing for purpose	English-language opportunities	Ongoing language teaching
	The Oxford Treasury of Classic Poems iF *Poems* (as a book or app)		1. Poems about war (e.g. *For the Fallen* by Laurence Binyon, *Dulce et Decorum Est* by Wilfrid Owen and *Here Dead We Lie* by A. E. Hausman) 2. Well-known poetry (e.g. *Ozymandias* by Percy Bysshe Shelly, *The Road Not Taken* by Robert Frost, *If* by Rudyard Kipling, *He Wishes for the Cloths of Heaven* by W. B. Yeats, or *Dream Variations* and *Final Curve* by Langston Hughes)		

(Continued)

English – Year 6 (continued)

Unit	Example texts	Ongoing outcomes	Writing for purpose	English-language opportunities	Ongoing language teaching
Poetry (1 week)	Children's own choice of poem	Performance of poem Hand-written version of poem for class anthology	**Persuade:** Short comment to accompany chosen poem explaining why everyone should read it **Discuss:** Personal responses to their chosen poem using different language forms showing understanding of ideas, language and themes		

Appendix II

The Labours of Hercules unit plan

Appendix II *The Labours of Hercules* unit plan

Shakespeare and More Text-based English unit	*The Labours of Hercules*	*Year 4*

Written outcomes:
A detailed character study of Hercules
and
An extended first-person narrative based on the story of *The Labours of Hercules*
Performance outcomes:
An oral retelling of one of Hercules' tasks

Key texts:
The Twelve Labours of Hercules by James Riordan and Christina Balit
Greek Heroes by Geraldine McCaughrean
Complementary texts:
Hercules by Fred van Lente
Greek Myths retold by Marcia Williams

Unit objectives (from the 2014 National Curriculum):

• Develop positive attitudes to reading and understanding of what they read
• Increase their familiarity with a wide range of key texts, including myths and legends
Specific teaching objectives (from the 2014 National Curriculum):

• Identify recurring themes and elements in different stories
• Draw inferences such as inferring characters' feelings, thoughts and motives from their actions
• Predict what might happen from details stated and implied in the text
• Recall and summarise main ideas from different parts of the text
• Plan their writing by:

– Discussing texts similar to the one they are planning to write in order to understand and learn from their structure, grammar and vocabulary
– Discussing and recording ideas for composition
• Draft and write by:

– Composing and rehearsing sentences orally (including dialogue), progressively building a varied and rich vocabulary and increasing range of sentence structures
– Shaping ideas into paragraphs
– Creating setting, characters and plot in narrative texts
• Evaluate and edit by:

– Assessing the effectiveness of their own and others' writing and suggesting improvements
– Proposing changes to grammar and vocabulary to improve consistency
– Proof-read for spelling and punctuation errors

Before you start:

- Elicit existing knowledge of the story and characters from the story (many children will be familiar with the popular Disney film *Hercules*, which borrows from a number of myths and legends)
- Discuss with children the world that the story is set in, linking to their knowledge of Ancient Greece – the Gods and the role of magic, dress and customs of the characters, technology available to characters, etc.
- Remind the children that although the Ancient Greeks were a real people who lived long ago, this story is a work of fiction told by them and then written down many years later

Session	Key learning objectives	Lesson content & organisation	Assessment
1	To be able to identify themes occurring in narratives To be able to listen to and demonstrate understanding of a text read aloud	Read to them/tell the class the start of *The Labours of Hercules*, with who Hercules was, who his parents were, and the background to how he found himself the servant of King Eurystheus. Discussion – who is Hercules and what do we know about him so far? Read/tell the class the first two tasks: The Nemean Lion and The Hydra of Lerna. Discuss what has happened and check everyone is following. Task: Class keep notes/framework for a story log that is to be completed over the course of the entire story. They record what happens in each labour, building to a picture of the whole story that will help them to plan their own writing.	Can the children identify themes occurring in narratives? Can they communicate this orally, drawing on evidence from the text to justify their opinions? Can the children demonstrate their understanding of the texts orally?
2	To infer characters' feelings, thoughts and motives from their action and dialogue	Read/tell the labour of The Augean Stables. Activity: Push the desks back or go to the hall for a drama activity. Pupils to work in groups to produce 3 tableaux images that tell the story. Share together as a class and evaluate. Discussion: What does the story tell you about Hercules? At some point before the next lesson, children write up their story logs.	Can the children infer characters' feelings, thoughts and motives from their action and dialogue?

(Continued)

Appendix II *The Labours of Hercules* unit plan (continued)

Session	Key learning objectives	Lesson content & organisation	Assessment
3	To retell narratives clearly and accurately To record ideas for composition	Today the children will continue the story. Task: In groups of 3–5, children are given one of five different labours: – The Ceryneian Deer – The Erymanthian Boar – The Stymphalian Birds – The Cretan Bull – The Horses of Diomedes Each group are given 15 minutes to prepare their story to present to the other groups. Members of the group then move to another group to present their story. By the end, all the children are familiar with the five stories and are 'experts' in one of them. At some point before the next lesson, children write up their story logs.	Can the children record their ideas for composition? Can the children retell narratives clearly and accurately?
4	To identify themes occurring in narratives, following discussion To be able to use paragraphs to organise ideas around a theme To infer characters' feelings, thoughts and motives from their action and dialogue	Read/tell the labour of 'The Girdle of Hippolyte. Discuss as a class: what does it tell us about Hercules? Why do the class think Hera is so determined to stop Hercules completing his tasks? Return and look at the structure of the book, noting where each child began reading. Analyse why the text was broken into paragraphs in the places it was. Discuss the purpose of paragraphs and how they aid a reader. Task: Children complete their story log. Read/tell the story of 'The Apples of the Hesperides. Discuss as a class. What does it tell us about Hercules? Why do you think this story would have been so popular with the Greeks? Have they met any of the other characters in it before? At some point before the next lesson, children write up their story logs.	Can the children identify themes occurring in narratives? Can they communicate this orally, drawing on evidence from the text to justify their opinions? Can the children identify where paragraphs have been used to organise ideas around a theme? Can the children infer characters' feelings, thoughts and motives from their action and dialogue?

Appendix II *The Labours of Hercules* unit plan (continued)

Session	Key learning objectives	Lesson content & organisation	Assessment
5	To draw conclusions about a character and support these with evidence from the text To understand how choices of vocabulary and grammar can change and enhance meaning To avoid ambiguity and repetition by choosing pronouns or nouns appropriately	Read/tell the final labour, The Underworld and the rest of the story until Hercules is released. Discuss the character of Hercules. How do we know what he is like? Discuss how he feels in different parts of the story. Pupils are given extracts from different versions of the story. Working in pairs or groups, children locate and highlight evidence in the texts that demonstrates what Hercules is like as a character. They can collect direct evidence from descriptions and make inferences from his words and actions. This can be recorded in a frame or in books. They then feedback to each other, sharing what they learned from their extract. These can be shared with the whole class. Tell class they will be writing the first draft of a character study of Hercules for homework. As a class, write a plan for what would be in a character study: • Description of the character (possibly appearance, definitely nature) • How we know this from the text	Can the children draw conclusions about a character and support these with evidence from the text? Can the children select an appropriate form for writing?
6	To assess the effectiveness of their own and others' writing, including tailoring improvements to needs of the reader To understand how to use apostrophes to mark singular and plural possession (e.g. *the girl's name, the boys' boots*)	Task: Children write character study of Hercules. Pupils read copies of one child's work that is strong, along with teacher feedback. Discussion: What are the strong/effective elements and the areas to strengthen? Repeat with a less-developed piece of work. Analyse strengths and share in table groups. Individually identify one area where improvements could be made. Discuss as class. Pupils consider their own work. Are any of the points made about other children's work applicable to their own? Children decide on changes they can make and share in groups.	Can the children assess the effectiveness of their own and others' writing, including tailoring improvements to needs of the reader?

(Continued)

Appendix II *The Labours of Hercules* unit plan (continued)

Session	Key learning objectives	Lesson content & organisation	Assessment
		Whole class teaching of apostrophes for singular and plural possession based on sentences drawn from children's work and invented sentences linked to this work. Include the case of 'Hercules' (singular), ending in a 's'. Model examples on board and ask children to write their own on whiteboards to demonstrate understanding. Children edit and then redraft work, paying particular attention to use of apostrophes. Work is collected in for written/detailed oral feedback.	
7	To record initial ideas for composition, drawing effectively from discussion of texts similar to the one they are planning to write	Explain to class that they are going to write their own version of *The Labours of Hercules* in which they will be the main character. The story will feature three labours they must undertake to receive forgiveness from the gods. The first step is to decide on a name for their character. Then the class can plan their own story. Class share story plans with one another in groups or as a whole class.	Can the children develop and communicate their ideas for composition? Can they draw effectively on discussion of texts similar to the one they are planning to write? Can the children communicate their ideas for narratives clearly and convincingly?
8	To use recorded ideas effectively to write descriptively	As a class, look at a photograph of a possible setting for one of Hercules' labours. This could be the cave where the Nemean Lion lives or King Eurystheus' castle. As a class, annotate the drawing, using effective descriptive language to translate the picture into words, modelling: – Similes and metaphors – Personification – Details drawn from sight, sound, scent and touch – Beautiful language Children draw or find their own pictures and then use this to write short piece of descriptive writing around the setting. Share these with groups or whole class, collecting particularly effective/beautiful language.	Can the children use recorded ideas effectively to write descriptively? Can the children make suggestions of words, phrases and ideas to create effective descriptive language?

Appendix II *The Labours of Hercules* unit plan (continued)

Session	Key learning objectives	Lesson content & organisation	Assessment
9	To draft simple setting, characters and plot in narrative texts To use inverted commas accurately to punctuate direct speech	Revise conventions for dialogue, including use of inverted commas for direct speech. Then show class some deliberately wrong examples. As a class, ask children to identify what is incorrect and then re-write correctly. Children to write some examples of their own that are correct on whiteboards and share with partner/class. Extended writing – Using their descriptive writing from yesterday and their story plans, class write their first labour. Children's first labour must be finished ready for tomorrow's lesson.	Can children draft simple setting, characters and plot in narrative texts? Can children use inverted commas accurately to punctuate direct speech?
10	To assess the effectiveness of their own and others' writing, including tailoring improvements to the needs of the reader To be able to use conventions for direct speech, correcting examples where errors have occurred in children's writing together on the whiteboard	Children work with the first draft of their labour from yesterday. With a partner, they read through, identifying areas where writing is particularly strong or effective vocabulary/language devices have been employed. Then discuss alterations that can be made – prompt children away from spelling and punctuation towards the language used. Pairs feedback to class about anything they thought was particularly good; these can be noted on the IWB. Revisit conventions for direct speech, correcting examples where errors have occurred in children's writing together on the whiteboard. Children edit their work. Work is collected in for detailed written/oral feedback. Homework: Children write first draft of the second labour.	Can the children assess the effectiveness of their own and others' writing, including tailoring improvements to needs of the reader?
11	To be able to use text structure, grammar and vocabulary to inform their own writing	Class have a few minutes to proofread their homework and check it is ready to hand in. Collect homework in and give brief oral feedback.	Can the children identify and discuss text structure, grammar and vocabulary and its effect on the reader? Can the children use this to inform their own writing?

(Continued)

Appendix II *The Labours of Hercules* unit plan (continued)

Session	Key learning objectives	Lesson content & organisation	Assessment
	To avoid ambiguity and repetition by choosing pronouns or nouns appropriately	As a class, consider text from The Labours of Hercules where Hercules kills the Nemean Lion. Discuss how writer uses language to convey action (short, punchy sentences, powerful verbs, dramatic sentence openings, the impression of violence, but not a great deal of gory detail). Pupils use whiteboards to contribute to whole-class shared writing for the slaying of the hydra. During this task remind children of need to make appropriate choices of pronoun, noun or noun phrase to avoid ambiguity and repetition. Model this through shared writing. Class return to their own draft of labour two and work to improve it, both in the light of oral feedback and the whole class shared writing. Work is collected in for detailed written feedback.	Can the children make appropriate choices of pronouns or nouns to avoid ambiguity and repetition?
12	To be able to use inference to inform reading and writing (such as inferring characters' feelings, thoughts and motives from their actions)	Show pupils two sentences where Hercules is afraid: one where it says so literally and one where it is inferred through actions. Discuss devices for showing emotion through inference (speech, actions, description, and rhetorical questions). In pairs, one child acts out emotion and other has to guess what this is. Bring a pair out to front and let class guess. As class to write a few sentences telling us how character is feeling. In books or using frame, pupils write a sentence using each of the techniques. Share sentences as a class and discuss their effectiveness.	Can the children infer information about a character (and their feelings, thoughts and motives) from a text?
13	To be able to create setting, characters and plot in narrative texts	Using examples from the text, identify where the author uses fronted adverbials (word, phrase or clause) to begin a sentence. Discuss why this feature is being used in each case (e.g. manner/degree [quickly, very] time [later that day, next], spatial [back at the palace, here] etc.) and discuss its effectiveness.	Can the children understand how fronted adverbials can be used effectively in writing? Can the children create setting, characters and plot in narrative texts effectively?

Appendix II *The Labours of Hercules* unit plan (continued)

Session	Key learning objectives	Lesson content & organisation	Assessment
	To understand how fronted adverbials can be used effectively in writing To use commas after fronted adverbials	Teach children the specific rule about use of commas. Children to write their own examples of adverbials to begin sentences the teacher shares as an example (e.g. … *Hercules ran towards the beast*). Discuss the purpose for each example. Extended writing – Using their story plans, notes on writing inferred emotion from yesterday and any other resources they have used so far, class write the final labour of their adventures. Children's final labour must be finished ready for tomorrow's lesson.	
14	To assess the effectiveness of their own and others' writing, tailoring improvements to needs of the reader To understand how fronted adverbials can be used effectively in writing To use commas after fronted adverbials	Collect written work in and give brief feedback. Pupils read copies of one child's work that is strong, along with teacher feedback. Discussion: What are the strong/effective elements and what are the areas that could be improved? Repeat with a less-developed piece of work. Analyse strengths and share in table groups. Individually identify one area where improvements could be made. Discuss as class. Ask the class to share examples where they have used fronted adverbials in their writing. Identify the purpose for this. Discuss how effective each is and, if necessary, re-draft together on board. Model an invented example where every sentence begins with an adverbial and discuss the effect of overuse. Children consider their own work in the light of this, adding examples or making corrections. Children edit their work, making changes as necessary. Work is collected in for detailed written feedback.	Can the children assess the effectiveness of their own and others' writing, including tailoring improvements to needs of the reader?

(Continued)

Appendix II *The Labours of Hercules* unit plan (continued)

Session	Key learning objectives	Lesson content & organisation	Assessment
15	To understand structure, grammar and vocabulary of book 'blurb' (to inform own writing)	Explain to class that they will be publishing their writing into books. As a class, identify key elements of fiction texts (front cover, blurb etc.) and what make them attractive to readers (presentation, clear text, illustrations) and write these up into success criteria. In groups, look at blurb for some published books and discuss. Draw out elements that are effective. Write blurb for book on board as a class, 'borrowing' effective language from books. Task: Children write a blurb for their own book.	Can the children understand structure, grammar and vocabulary of book 'blurb'? Can they use this inform own writing?
16	To work productively with others to assess the effectiveness of their own and others' writing	Children begin process of publishing their book, checking back to ensure they have all elements: – Front Cover (title, author, illustration) – Chapter 1 (with illustrations if desired) – Chapter 2 (with illustrations if desired) – Chapter 3 (with illustrations if desired) – Back Cover (with blurb) Over several days, they will redraft each chapter of the book, produce illustrations and make the front and back covers. Share examples of quality work so far, encouraging pupils to borrow ideas from one another. When publication is finished, books can be swapped and read by other children, perhaps writing book reviews of one another's books. They can be displayed and or presented in a class assembly, where children read from them. At the end of the project, return to *The Labours of Hercules* and read/tell children the story of Hercules' marriage to Deianeira, battle with Nessus and the ending from *Greek Heroes* by Geraldine McCaughrean.	

Appendix III

Recommended books

The following list of recommended books has been compiled while working in schools across the UK: talking to children, teachers and librarians. An up-to-date version can be found by visiting: www.shakespeare andmore.com/greatbooks

This list is by no means exhaustive – there are too many wonderful children's books out there for any list to even scratch the surface and every reader will have their own preferences. Great teachers of English are readers, so go out and explore the world of children's literature: it is necessary if you want to teach by the book.

Picturebooks for everyone

A Bit Lost by Chris Haughton
A Child of Books by Oliver Jeffers and Sam Winston
A Friend for Little Bear by Harry Horse
Again by Emily Gravett
Beegu by Alexis Deacon
Chalk by Bill Thomson
Christopher Nibble by Charlotte Middleton
Courtney by John Burningham
Dogger by Shirley Hughes
Du Iz Tak? by Carson Ellis
Edgar Gets Ready for Bed by Jennifer Adams
Flotsam by David Weisner
Frog and Toad books by Arnold Lobel

Funnybones by Janet and Allan Ahlberg
Good Little Wolf by Nadia Shireen
Grandad's Island by Benji Davies
Hairy Maclary by Lynley Dodd
Have You Seen Elephant? by David Barrow
Hermelin by Mini Grey
Hogwash by Arthur Geisert
Hoot Owl – Master of Disguise by Sean Taylor
I Really Want to Eat a Child by Sylvianne Donnio
Instructions by Neil Gaiman
Journey by Aaron Becker
Kicking a Ball by Allan Ahlberg
Lionheart by Richard Collingridge
Lost and Found by Oliver Jeffers
Max by Marc Martin
Mr Gumpy's Outing by John Burningham
Mr Tiger Goes Wild by Peter Brown
Mr Wolf's Pancakes by Jan Fernley
Mr Wuffles by David Weisner
Not Now, Bernard by David McKee
Odd Dog Out by Rob Biddulph
Oh No, George! by Chris Haughton
Oi Dog! by Kes Gray and Jim Field
Oi Frog! by Kes Gray and Jim Field
On Sudden Hill by Linda Sarah and Benji Davies
On the Way Home by Jill Murphy
Open Very Carefully by Nick Bromley
Owl Babies by Martin Waddell
Peace at Last by Jill Murphy
Peepo! by Janet and Allan Ahlberg
Penguin in Peril by Helen Hancocks
Puffin Peter by Petr Horacek
Rain by Sam Usher
Rosie's Walk by Pat Hutchins
Shh, We Have a Plan! by Chris Haughton
Sloth Slept On by Frann Preston-Gannon
Slow Loris by Alexis Deacon
Solomon Crocodile by Catherine Rayner
Speckle the Spider by Emma Dodson
Steven Seagull: Action Hero by Elys Dolan
Super Happy Magic Forest by Matt y Long
The Book with No Pictures by BJ Novak
The Cat from Hunger Mountain by Ed Young

The Crocodile Who Didn't Like Water by Gemma Merino
The Day the Crayons Quit by Drew Drywalt
The Deep Dark Wood by Algy Craig Hall
The Dot by Peter H Reynolds
The Forest Child by Richard Edwards
The Green Ship by Quentin Blake
The Jolly Postman by Janet and Alan Ahlberg
The Lighthouse Keeper's Lunch by Rhonda and David Armitage
The Selfish Crocodile by Faustin Charles
The Storm Whale by Benji Davies
The Tiger Who Came to Tea by Judith Kerr
The True Story of Three Little Pigs by Jon Scieszka
The Very Hungry Caterpillar by Eric Carle
The Wolf's Story by Toby Forward
The Wolves in the Walls by Neil Gaiman
The Yes by Sarah Bee
There is a Tribe of Kids by Lane Smith
This is Not My Hat by Jon Klassen
Traction Man is Here by Mini Grey
Tuesday by David Wiesner
We Found a Hat by John Klassen
We're Going on a Bearhunt by Michael Rosen
Weasels by Elys Dolan
Where the Wild Things Are by Maurice Sendak
Would You Rather . . . by John Burningham

Picturebooks for older readers

Black Dog by Levi Pinfold
FArTHER by Graham Baker-Smith
Fungus the Bogeyman by Raymond Briggs
Hare by Zoe Greaves and Leslie Sadleir
Hilda and the Troll by Luke Pearson
House Held up by Trees by Ted Kooser and Jon Klassen
How to Live Forever by Colin Thompson
I am the Mummy Heb-Nerfert by Eve Bunting
Little Red by Bethan Woollvin
Mr Wuffles by David Wiesner
Night of the Gargoyles by Eve Bunting
The Arrival by Shaun Tan
The Island by Armin Greder

The Mysteries of Harris Burdick by Chris van Allsburg
The Paperbag Prince by Colin Thompson
The Rabbits by John Marsden and Shaun Tan
The Watertower by Gary Crew and Steven Woolman
Weslandia by Paul Fleischman

Traditional tales and retellings of classics

Aesop's Fables retold by Alice Shirley
Aladdin and the Enchanted Lamp retold by Philip Pullman
Anansi Stories from *Tales from the West Indies* by Faustin Charles
Atticus the Storyteller's 100 Greek Myths by Lucy Coats
Beowulf retold by Kevin Crossley-Holland
Collected Folk Tales by Alan Garner
Dragon Mountain by Tim Vyner
Fairy Tales told by Berlie Doherty
Gawain and the Green Knight retold by Philip Reeve
Greek Heroes by Geraldine McCaughrean
Greek Myths by Ann Turnbull
Greek Myths retold by Marcia Williams
Grimm Tales by Philip Pullman
Mother Goose's Playtime Rhymes by Axel Scheffler
Myths and Legends retold by Anthony Horowitz
One Thousand and One Arabian Nights retold by Geraldine McCaughrean
Robin Hood and a World of Other Stories by Geraldine McCaughrean
Robin of Sherwood by Michael Morpurgo
Selkie by Gillan McClure
Shakespeare Stories by Leon Garfield
Shakespeare Stories II by Leon Garfield
Stories from *A River of Stories* compiled by Alice Curry and Jan Pienkowski
Stories from Shakespeare by Geraldine McCaughrean
Tales of Ancient Egypt by Roger Lancelyn Green
The Adventures of Odysseus by Hugh Lupton and Daniel Morden
The Arabian Nights by Michael Foreman
The Brave Sister retold by Fiona Waters
The House of Cats by Maggie Pearson
The Iliad and The Odyssey retold by Marcia Williams
The Odyssey Graphic Novel by Gareth Hinds
The Odyssey retold by Robin Lister
The Once and Future King by TH White
The Orchard Book of Shakespeare Stories by Andrew Matthews

The Orchard Book of Swords, Sorcerers and Superheroes by Tony Bradman
The Oxford Treasury of Fairy Tales by Geraldine McCaughrean
The Seven Voyages of Sinbad the Sailor retold by John Yeoman
The Sword and the Circle by Rosemary Sutcliff
The Thousand Nights and One Night retold by David Walser and Jan Pienkowski
The Twelve Labours of Heracles by James Ford
Trick of the Tale by John and Caitlin Matthews

Classic children's literature

Carrie's War by Nina Bawden
Charlotte's Web by E. B. White
Emil and the Detectives by Erich Kästner
George's Marvellous Medicine by Roald Dahl
Goodnight Mr Tom by Michelle Magorian
How the Whale Became by Ted Hughes
Just So Stories by Rudyard Kipling
Kidnapped by Robert Louis Stevenson
Lord of the Flies by William Golding
The Adventures of Sherlock Holmes by Sir Arthur Conan Doyle
The BFG by Roald Dahl
The Call of the Wild by Jack London
The Eagle of the Ninth by Rosemary Sutcliff
The Hobbit by J. R. R. Tolkien
The Iron Man by Ted Hughes
The Little Prince by Antoine de Saint-Exupéry
The Memoirs of Sherlock Holmes by Sir Arthur Conan Doyle
The War of the Worlds by H. G. Wells
The Weirdstone of Brisingamen by Alan Garner
The Wind in the Willows by Kenneth Grahame
The Wizard of Earthsea by Ursula Le Guin
The Wolves of Willoughby Chase by Joan Aiken
Treasure Island by Robert Louis Stevenson
Watership Down by Richard Adams

Poetry collections

Cautionary Verses by Hilaire Belloc
Classic Poetry selected by Michael Rosen
Collected Poems for Children by Ted Hughes

iF – A Treasury of Poems for Almost Every Possibility edited by Allie Esiri and Rachel Kelly
New and Collected Poems for Children by Carol Anne Duffy
Revolting Rhymes by Roald Dahl
The Nation's Favourite Children's Poems – BBC Books
The Oxford Treasury of Classic Poems
The Rattle Bag edited by Seamus Heaney and Ted Hughes
The Ring of Words by Roger McGough
Where my Wellies Take Me by Clare and Michael Morpurgo

Beautiful non-fiction

A Dictionary of Monsters and Mysterious Beasts by Carey Miller
Atlas of Animal Adventures by Rachel Williams, Emily Hawkins and Lucy Letherland
Enormous Smallness by Matthew Burgess
Exotic Animals A–Z by Marc Martin
Fantastically Great Women Who Changed the World by Kate Pankhurst
Gravity by Jason Chin
How to Keep Dinosaurs by Robert Mash
Magnificent Creatures: Animals on the move by Anna Wright
Mythological Monsters of Ancient Greece by Sara Fanelli
On Beam of Light by Jennifer Berne (about Albert Einstein)
Professor Stewart's Cabinet of Mathematical Curiosities by Iain Stewart
Star Stuff by Stephanie Roth Sisson
The *Little People, Big Dreams* series
The Magic of Reality by Richard Dawkins
The Man Who Walked Between the Towers by Mordecai Gerstein
The Number Devil by Hans Magnus Enzenberger
The Usborne History of Britain
The Wonder Garden by Kristina S Williams and Jenny Broom
What Makes Me? By Robert Winston
Wholly Irresponsible Experiments by Sean Connolly
You are Stardust by Elin Kelsey and Soyeon Kim

Contemporary novels for children

A Monster Calls by Patrick Ness
Clockwork by Philip Pullman
Cogheart by Peter Bunzl

Coraline by Neil Gaiman
Coram Boy by Jamila Gavin
Diamond Brothers books by Anthony Horowitz
Flat Stanley by Jeff Brown
Fly by Night by Frances Hardinge
Freak the Mighty by Rodman Philbrick
His Dark Materials books by Philip Pullman
Holes by Louis Sachar
Kensuke's Kingdom by Michael Morpurgo
Lyra's Oxford by Philip Pullman
Mango and Bambang by Polly Faber and Clara Vulliamy
Montmorency by Eleanor Updale
Mortal Engines by Philip Reeve
Mouse Bird Snake Wolf by David Almond
My Brother's Ghost by Alan Ahlberg
Not the End of the World by Geraldine McCaughrean
Odd and the Frost Giants by Neil Gaiman
Once by Morris Gleitzman
Once Upon a Time in the North by Philip Pullman
Pugs of the Frozen North by Philip Reeve and Sarah McIntyre
Raymie Nightingale by Kate DiCamillo
Ribblestrop by Andy Mulligan
Rooftoppers by Katherine Rundell
The Firework-Maker's Daughter by Philip Pullman
The Girl of Ink and Stars by Kiran Millwood Hargrave
The Graveyard Book by Neil Gaiman
The Imaginary by AF Harrold
The Last Polar Bears by Harry Horse
The Many Worlds of Albie Bright by Christopher Edge
The Miraculous Journey of Edward Tulane by Kate DiCamillo
The Twits by Roald Dahl
The Various by Steve Augarde
Uncle Montague's Tales of Terror by Chris Priestly
Wonder by R. J. Palaciao

For regularly updated book recommendations, visit: www.shakespeare
andmore.com/greatbooks

Index